We Have Moved Mountains

From South Africa to the USA

by

Christian S. Gerber

Bloomington, IN  Milton Keynes, UK

authorHOUSE

AuthorHouse™
1663 Liberty Drive, Suite 200
Bloomington, IN 47403
www.authorhouse.com
Phone: 1-800-839-8640

AuthorHouse™ UK Ltd.
500 Avebury Boulevard
Central Milton Keynes, MK9 2BE
www.authorhouse.co.uk
Phone: 08001974150

First published by AuthorHouse 6/22/2006

ISBN: 1-4259-2826-9 (sc)

Printed in the United States of America
Bloomington, Indiana

This book is printed on acid-free paper.

Dedicated to my wife Karen, children Natalie, Wayne and Melissa for their unwavering support and trust in my leadership.

A special word of thanks to Karen who helped in editing this book.

Foreword

By Norman Flynn

I esteem it a great honor to write a foreword to this book that tells about faith, hope and love of God by the Gerber Family.

I have known Chris, Karen and their family for twenty-four years.

As a family, they decided to emigrate to the United States of America. All the odds of them getting here were against them.

I know they were asking God to help them. Many prayers were worded by them and others. But their faith for this to materialize was undaunted.

Chris gave up a good position at the bank in South Africa, also a good living, but there were signs on the horizon that he could see and did not like.

This was a gigantic step for them as a family to take, but their trust was in God. Their prayers were answered after months of negotiating.

Joyce and I went to the airport to welcome them to the U.S.A.

Introduction

Why would anyone want to give up a career that took him years to build, and provided good income and security?

Why would anyone leave their land of birth, family and friends, and venture into a strange land with so many unknown factors and insecurities?

The Gerber Family, Chris, Karen, Natalie, Wayne and Melissa, did just that. We left South Africa in 1995 to settle in the United States of America.

This book is firstly about our country South Africa. We were born in a land with many diversities and struggles. We inherited one of the most hated forms of government in the world and the difficulties of correcting it.

Then we share with you our dreams, visions, goals, and the deep waters we were prepared to go through to reach them.

It took us 25 years to achieve our goal. We had our dreams, and it all finally came together for us. Keeping our eyes focused on God and allowing Him to guide and direct us, turned out to be the best strategy that anyone could have. He blessed and tried us, yet we always knew that He was in control and there was nothing we could do other than to trust Him and let Him know that. We still do today.

We are not perfect human beings, and have many sins and shortcomings. God is Almighty, and as weak as we are, we believe in Him and have laid our weaknesses at His feet and trust Him with our souls.

The Gerbers live at 20661 AL.Hwy 117, Ider, AL. 35981. Our phone number is 256-632-9157. If you, the reader, would like to talk to us, we would gladly share our experiences with you and maybe, just maybe, we can help you understand how real God is.

CONTENTS

PART 1

1. SOUTH AFRICA - THE LAND OF APARTHEID   3

2. HOW DID WE GET HERE?   7

3. THE EARLY DAYS OF MY LIFE   13

4. THE RELIGION OF OUR FATHERS   21

5. THE PEOPLE WE MET DAILY   27

6. PERCEPTIONS OR FACTS   33

7. WHITE SOUTH AFRICAN POLITICS   39

8. CONTROL VERSUS FREEDOM   45

9. THE WORK ENVIRONMENT   49

10. SOUTH AFRICAN MILITARY   53

11. SOUTH AFRICAN POLICE   57

12. THE NEW SOUTH AFRICA   59

CONTENTS (Cont.)
PART 2

1. THE EARLY YEARS 65

2. THE FIRST TRIP OVERSEAS 71

3. THE PRESSURE GETS WORSE 77

4. THE OPPORTUNITY ARRIVES 83

5. THE DAY OF THE INTERVIEW 91

6. GETTING OUR GREEN CARDS 95

7. THE LAST TWO MONTHS 105

8. ACCOMMODATION FOR ONE MONTH 113

9. WE ARE LEAVING SOUTH AFRICA 121

10. THE FIRST SIX MONTHS IN A FOREIGN LAND 125

11. GOD TEACHES US HUMILITY 137

12. LOOKING BACK 145

13. LOOKING AHEAD 147

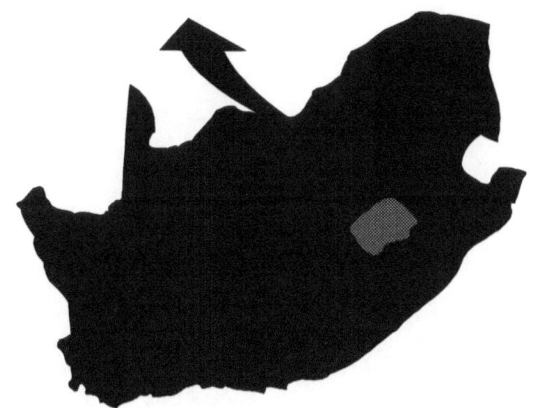

PART 1

THE LAND OF OUR FOREFATHERS

CHAPTER 1

SOUTH AFRICA -
THE LAND OF APARTHEID

South Africa, situated at the southern most tip of Africa, has more to offer in natural beauty and mineral riches than most other countries. For those that had the privilege to visit this fabulous land, the experience must have been breathtaking and eventful.

Yet, instead of these attractions being known worldwide and eagerly sought after by tourists, the country will rather be remembered for the minority rule of the white people and a system called "apartheid".

The system of apartheid made a major contribution in keeping visitors away. Worldwide sanctions against the ruling government discouraged many prospective visitors and investment seekers.

Thank God, that system belongs to the past.

This period of time has so damaged the image of white South Africans all over the world that it may take a few generations to heal these deep wounds. Along with the apartheid lifestyle came the nasty accusations of "racism".

White South Africans are not all racists. Many of them were victims of a culture and system that was put in place before their birth. Many inherited this stigma just like all Russians were seen as communists.

The end of apartheid meant freedom and democracy for all "non-white" people in the country. Generations of blacks and colored people were left behind during a period of tremendous growth in the country. They were excluded from compulsory education programs and had no vote in a country where they lived all their generations. Forced separation limited their options of obtaining property.

So we voted to try and start over to correct that.

It may sound strange, but it also meant a certain freedom for the majority of whites. They were freed from a culture of discrimination and relieved from the burden of the unfair society they inherited.

No, I am not excusing the current generation from the guilt of this system. Something could have been done years ago. However, just like it will take years to change the lifestyles of people in Iraq to live as spontaneous, free people, it took years for the current South African generation to understand the impact of the apartheid system and to take action to change it.

I was born under apartheid. I was one of the 68% white voters who chose to follow F.W. de Klerk to scrap the system and have a free and fair South Africa. We were all delighted when the referendum results were announced and even more so when the first free elections were held in 1994. We stood in lines with people of all colors to vote and all of a sudden we were ready to share our homeland. It was like a big load was taken off our backs.

The results were great but unfortunately, in South Africa, untested. Yes, we were still skeptical about the final result. Even today, many South Africans are not at ease with the new South Africa. No, they do not regret the free South Africa, but experiences in other countries like Zimbabwe, remind them of similar changes that went horribly wrong. The older generation will find it harder to adapt and to adjust their thinking.

It is not the sharing of the country and all its resources that is the problem. It may not even be a black/white issue.

The issue is the difference in cultures and religions. This has also been exaggerated by the multiplicity of ethnic groups and cultures within the country. The problem can be summed up in one word: mistrust.

Then there is still the threat of possible retribution. Our human nature can always justify revenge. "The whites must get what they deserve".

Most white South Africans will probably be comfortable with some form of affirmative action. Retribution may be viewed in a much different light. Any discriminatory or depressive action from non-white governments will automatically give justification to the white people to defend apartheid. So, two wrongs never make a right and for South Africa to be a prosperous, free society, the government (black or white) has the responsibility to make it happen.

5

South Africans want freedom, peace and harmony just like any one else on earth. Hopefully that will happen and future generations in that beautiful country may live to see that materialize.

My family and I left this beautiful country for our own personal reasons, but we will always remain loyal to our land of birth. We visit as often as our finances will allow because we have loving family members and friends there; also because the country and everything that make it so special and beautiful, is in our blood.

CHAPTER 2.

HOW DID WE GET HERE?

South Africa is bordered by ocean on three sides and it is at Cape Point or as more commonly known, "Cape of Storms" or "Cape of Good Hope", where the cold water from the Atlantic Ocean meets the warmer water of the Indian Ocean.

The question of how we got there can best be answered by the historians. How did white people land up in a country or for that matter, a continent that is predominantly populated by black people?

I was born there; on August 23, 1949, shortly after the end of the Second World War. I was born in a small village known as Olifantshoek, near George in the Cape Province.

My father was born there; and his father, and his father - quite a number of generations. I have never managed to trace the total family tree but that was never all that important to me. I am a man who lives for the present and dream about the future. The past has never mattered all that much – unless of course it haunts you or requires clarification.

Fortunately for me, I have no reason to have to explain my heritage to anyone. Thinking about it, I do not believe it can be required of anyone on earth. It is not where we come from that matters but it is what we do while we live our lives. Most of us are born into situations and environments that we have absolute no control over and which we could not change even if we wanted to.

However, a little insight in our family history may provide some understanding of our outlook on life and the reason why we have operated in a certain way. White South Africans have been tagged as racists, monster-like creatures who have no love, compassion or feelings. We have been labeled as selfish and inhumane.

Yes, I am one of those. No, I do not agree with those tags, but my opinion may not amount to much.

So, back to the original question – how did we get there?

History tells us of great explorers like Vasco da Gama and Bartholemew Diaz that first traveled around the bottom tip of Africa. They landed there for fresh water and other needs, but never settled there.

That part of Africa was already highly populated by numerous black ethnic groups as well as Khoi, Griquas and San. The latter three groups were all of a lighter skin color and like the black ethnic groups spoke their own individual ethnic languages.

It was the Dutch under Jan van Riebeeck who first landed in Cape Town in 1652 with the purpose of settling there. The Dutch saw strategic benefits in the Cape sea route. They were merchants carrying spices from the East Indian Islands. The Suez Canal was built many years later and the Cape route provided the necessary halfway station for fresh water and food.

My family must have had some Dutch heritage, for Dutch was the only language my grandparents ever spoke. My dad was a Gerber, Swiss-German, and my mom was a Botha, French. Their ancestors must have married into the Dutch heritage somehow, because nobody in our family ever spoke either German or French.

There were however French Huguenots and Germans who also settled in Cape Province not long after the Dutch.

The Reformation movement in Europe was one of the main reasons for Europeans leaving their homes to find a home somewhere else.

The Reformation movement originated because individuals in Europe started studying the Bible for themselves. Today, we all recognize and value such freedom. Yet, for them their religious aspirations and freedoms became nightmares. Instead of being able to worship their God in peace, they were threatened by the Catholics in their own countries. The threats were of such a nature that these people were prepared to give up their own homelands and things they have worked for all their lives just to have peace.

They were Christians or trying to be and were ready to live lives as defined by Jesus Christ. They recognized God as the Creator and were ready to worship Him and Him only, loving their neighbors as He instructed them. Yet, their neighbors seemed to be uninterested in their peaceful nature and persecuted them for the fact that they dared to have their own faith.

Is that not absolutely cruel? Or is cruelty only recognized when we have nothing to lose when we denounce it? It is so typical of the world we live in. We can all justify our own iniquities whether we are right or not. The stronger my position, the easier it seems for me to get away with atrocities.

What person has the right to dictate to anyone else how to worship God Almighty? The words "crucify Him" seem to ring in the back of my mind.

Leaving your own country to move to a foreign land is not something that one does lightly. There are major costs involved, but the financial impacts have nothing on the emotional and sentimental values offered. I have done this not so long ago with my own family and for my own reasons, and I know how it feels.

I sometimes wonder how those that fight for so-called human rights have viewed these facts of history. Has it been forgotten? Or is it perhaps that one should not speak against it in fear of persecution similar to that of the 15th century?

Yes, my ancestors did not leave their land to occupy someone else's. They left because by their calculation, they had no choice. They left Europe with the goal of protecting their religion and culture and were prepared to pay whatever cost was necessary to achieve that.

When they arrived in South Africa, there were no hotels, hospitals and highways waiting on them to assist them in an easy settlement. In contrast, just like those that moved to America, found an undeveloped country with many dangers and discomforts.

There were no kinfolk or friends ready to welcome them and serve them meals - only a barren land with uncivilized occupants who were ready to kill on sight. I suppose they were intruders, just like everyone who explored and decided to settle in a foreign land.
They did not leave their fatherland to go and conquer and occupy. Their intentions were never to subject and enslave any other nation. They fled their own countries because their right to follow their own faith was taken from them. So they left and landed in a wild and dangerous place.

Those were the conditions that met them in Africa. They found themselves in a position where they had to make it on their own to survive. No federal government to assist them and protect their rights. They were really no better off than in the countries they left, except for the fact that they had religious freedom – vitally important to them as it is to me.

So these peace-loving, God-fearing people found themselves again in a situation where they were threatened. Only this time it was not because of their religion, but because they were white and they were foreigners.

They were on a continent where survival of the fittest was part of the daily procedures. If you did not have the means or the know-how of how to protect you and your family, your chance of survival was slim!

Many of the settlers left the coastal areas to explore the rest of the country. In 1838 a great number left on an inland trek where they met the major black tribes. Many conflicts occurred during this movement north.

Once settled in what were then the Transvaal and Free State provinces, they established their own republics. It was also in these provinces where gold was discovered in 1881. It was also here where the conflict with the reigning British government, who was by now ruling the Cape and Natal provinces as colonies, resulted in the Boer Wars. They were finally conquered in 1901 and in 1910 the Union of South Africa was established under British rule.

CHAPTER 3.

THE EARLY DAYS OF MY LIFE

Olifantshoek is only 15 miles from George, the nearest biggish town. Situated between Outeniqua Mountain and the sea, this is surely one of the most beautiful places on earth. We never really recognized it those days because it was part of our every day life and we hardly ever got to see any other part of our own country.

We lived about 5 miles from the sea and very often walked that distance to go fishing.

O, yes, we had to walk it. There were very few families during my childhood years that had the luxury of an automobile. In fact, I could possibly count the number of vehicles registered in our area on my fingers alone.

That reminds me of one of the hobbies we as children had. We each kept note of the registration number of vehicles we saw. Our objective was to see who could compile the longest list. Today, that will be a silly conquest because of the numerous cars on the road.

However, I doubt whether my list, compiled over a year, had any more than 50 – 100 numbers on it – and that would include the days we went to town!

We were poor people. It took us years before we had the joy of luxury items that other nations, some of them European, were accustomed to. I think that we got our first radio when I was already in high school. We all used to go and visit my uncle whenever there was a rugby match played by our provincial or national teams. The reception was not very good, but adults and kids alike were glued to the only radio available to follow the achievements of our favorite sport teams.

There was no electricity. We had no running water. We had no inside toilet facilities. We did not frown upon such things as "outhouses" because it was part of our lives and a necessity as well. As young boy I often had to clean it and that was even more unpleasant than to use it. It is amazing what one can get use to when the options are limited!

We gathered rainwater in tanks from our guttering system. It was in the 1960's before a water pipeline was close enough for us to have a tap or water faucet on our property. It was hard carrying a ten-gallon bucket of water and more often than not, we would spill half of it by the time we reach home.

Our bath water had to be boiled on a wood stove. That would take quite a while to heat and we all had to be patient in waiting our turns. There were no electrical light switches and we found candles and oil lamps as part of our every day "appliances".

This simple lighting system was often a greater blessing than a hindrance. We were not accustomed to the fancy stuff found in cities, so we never missed it. Our parents used the time after a hard days labor to teach us about life. We learned about God, read the Bible together and each had a chance to pray. We learned about our forefathers and about the tragedies of wars and famine. They taught us the value of dignity, self respect and honor.

Yes, our parents used our simple lifestyle to enrich us with the most precious attributes of humanity. They never instilled in us anything ugly or nasty to other people. My parents did not teach us any rule that was not the same for all of our neighbors, whether they were white, black or in between. Every person was a creation of God and according to our Bible, Jesus died for each individual without favoritism.

The word "right" was never something we were taught to claim for ourselves. We accepted the fact that we were all simple, fallible human beings on a planet that we sincerely believed was created by a supreme God and our purpose was to fear Him and keep His commandments. We knew we would make mistakes and even sin. Yet our desire was to live in peace and harmony with everyone – even with those of different color, culture and creed.

My father would have given me a thrashing if I ever treated any older person with disrespect. Again, color or creed did not make a difference. Our culture demanded kindness and respect for fellow human beings and my father, although not highly educated, was a man with great insight and character. He understood the values of life and he also understood his role as father. His only goal in life was to please his God and to teach his family to do the same. Discrimination against another group of people was not part of our teaching and I think it shocked us in latter years when we discovered that we were part of a system that was unfair.

But more of that later.

He and my mother managed to reach standard 6 or grade 8 before they had to leave school and help to earn a living for their respective families. Taking care of cattle, chopping wood for cooking food and washing dishes were only some of the chores that they and even us got used to and never dared complain about. They were both pretty smart people, but there were no money for further schooling and their education never went any further.

So, along with this lack of college education there were the disadvantages of limited job selection. My parents had to make the best of the jobs they could find and worked at it as if it was the greatest opportunity in life. The salaries were hardly enough to feed the family, but the family values made us rich people. We had one another and our faith and to us there was never anything on earth more valuable or precious.

I cannot remember my mother ever complaining about these discomforts in her life. She was a woman like any other and appreciated the things that woman value and long for just like any other. My mother had a job in a grocery store and cycled there and back every day for as long as I can remember. The roads were gravel and were only tarred shortly before I left high school. There were no special tracks for bicycles and the two miles my mother cycled every day, was difficult at times.

So we as kids grew up learning about the values of life and human relations rather than science and technology. To us those subjects belong with the clever people in the cities – those rich and powerful people with the fancy motorcars.

Working in my father's garden was not my only task as a youngster. My dad worked for the forestry department and for the first 10-12 years of my life he cycled to work and back every day. The sawmill they worked at was about 5 miles away and there was no public transportation. So my dad had to get up early in the morning, 4:30am to be exact, in order to reach work on time. It was my job to get up before him and prepare coffee for his thermo flask and to get the fire in the stove on the go for the coming day. I got up every morning at 4:15am from Monday to Friday from the age of ten till I finished high school in 1967.

Saturdays and Sundays were a little easier. I only had to get up at about 6:30am to milk a cow or two. The fire still had to be made – did I mention that it was my responsibility to find all the necessary thin wood and sticks with which to start the fire?

My two older sisters did the same before I was big enough to take on this responsibility. There was no time for parents to feel sorry for their poor little children. Life was tough, but hard work never killed or shamed those who understood principles of responsibility.

Chopping wood was another chore. I had to handle a man's axe when I was only 6 years old. I think my mother was a little bit concerned at first, but I never chopped off any part of my body and so she accepted my growing-up challenges as I did. I have to admit however that she had lots of reason to be concerned because that axe was nearly as big as I.

This seemingly difficult life was filled with many blessings. Issues such as stress were not common to us. We were poor and yet never worried about tomorrow. Every day had its own issues, but we managed and the family and community provided enough love and security. We never expected to become rich or famous. Yes, as kids we had our dreams and aspirations and often our parents would see great futures for us, but a lot of it was pie in the sky.

When I reached standard 6, I had to go to a boarding school about 15 miles from our home. I lived in that boarding house for 5 years with about 80 other white boys. We lived under very strict disciplinary rules and were only allowed to go home every three weeks. This all sound very tough but it is in this place where I learned to stand on my own feet. I had to work carefully with the little pocket money my parents gave me and making my own bed never killed me.

The children of this generation may find this as shocking news, but in our days those things were accepted as part of life and we look back at it with great appreciation of the values we learned by it.

It was at boarding school where I learned of another of the South African diversities and the division that came with it. The white South Africans were predominantly Afrikaans speaking but there were also a great number English speaking people. These two groups had their own backgrounds and loyalties. The English speaking people did not approve of the National Party and most of them voted for the opposition United Party.

The predominantly Dutch settlers developed their own language and in 1925 "Afrikaans" became one of the official languages of the country. This language originated out of Dutch, German and other world languages. It stood on its own grammar rules and in 1933 the first Bible was translated into Afrikaans. This was great progress for a small nation and the language united them even more.

The Afrikaans speaking South Africans were the ones who fought against the British in the Anglo-Boer Wars and resented the English speaking for not supporting them in that struggle. The English speaking citizens did not support the breaking away from British rule when South Africa became a republic in 1961 and that divided these two groups further.

Ironically, my wife Karen was one of the English speaking South Africans while I had the Afrikaans heritage.

CHAPTER 4.

THE RELIGION OF OUR FATHERS

Most of the white people living in South Africa were Calvinists. Most of them were members of the Dutch Reformed Church that originated out of Europe. They believed in God Almighty and in Jesus Christ as the Messiah. They also believed in the Holy Spirit as the third personality of the Godhead.

They used the Bible in directing their faith. They believed that God created man and the universe.

They studied God's relationship with the patriarchs and with the children of Israel and tried to mold their own lives after the patterns of the Old Testament. God instructed the children of Israel to worship Him and Him only and my people held strongly to that principle. I have since then come to a different understanding of some of these Bible teachings but respect them for following their doctrines with great dedication.

It is this great dedication that may have caused some of their misunderstandings followed by very unfair laws.

God instructed the children of Israel to keep them pure and to stay away from other nations and their gods. He did not approve of any marriage to "strangers" knowing that it may lead to straying after other gods and idols. The Old Testament is full of stories where men of God strayed when they got involved with women from other nations. Both Samson and Solomon found it difficult to remain faithful to God once they followed after heathen women.

The church taught that the laws that God gave to the children of Israel, also applies just like that to any God-fearing group of people. So we believed that we should marry someone within our culture and color. The intent was not discrimination but rather a focus on a protection of culture and creed. There are still today many nations applying the same concept and for the same reasons. Dating across color lines or with people of other faith was therefore not only frowned upon, but strictly forbidden.

According to today's standards, that interfered with our rights as individuals. However, individual rights were valued less than the protection of the group and culture and what one would call a right today, was ignored and the status quo accepted without even a question.

We were proud to be part of a culture where God was feared and we knew that the world at large will not accept that and to tell the truth, it did not matter. World opinion would have let to our early destruction and so we found it necessary to follow our own faith and face the consequences.

Believing in a Creator is probably what eventually led to the scrapping of apartheid. If there was no God of creation, there would be no God after death either. If that be so, our own opinions and cultures become our own guidelines for this life and it does not really matter what others think. So in a world of "no God" apartheid would have been justifiable. In contrast, a faith in God includes considering a life defined by Him and a judgment in a life after death.

God would not approve of such a system.

Being at loggerheads with one's neighbor and the rest of the world was surely not the most comfortable feeling especially if you are a professing Christian. Every person's goal was to be loving and kind to his or her neighbor because that is the ultimate requirement of being a Christian. The dilemma was that every one else dictated their requirements and the result was conflict of interest.

These Dutch\German reformers, for that was what we were, did not plan on running again like their forefathers were forced to do. This time they had a home established and planned to fight for it until the bitter end. They were only outnumbered by the black ethnic groups and although it was not their first choice, were ready to do whatever it takes to survive.

So their faith is what kept them unified and that is how the motto "ex unitate virae" (unity is strength) found its way to the first South African flag. Unfortunately for the country, that unity was only valued by the white people as the rest of the inhabitants found us to be unwanted.

We did not understand these antagonistic feelings toward us because we were so indoctrinated and brainwashed by the teachings of the church and our traditions. Scriptures that were quoted never applied to us as a nation. The Old Testament scriptures only applied to the children of Israel, but we also wanted to be a special people for God and it was convenient to believe the preachers and church rulers who taught us so.

The church helped the white people to obtain properties and although they had to pay for it, got it reasonably cheaply. My parents got about 10 acres which was a portion of property that my grandparents acquired. I came to realize many years later that their relationship with the church must have allowed them certain privileges that the colored people, who were not part of the church membership, did not have. The colored people had their own congregation of the same faith, but there was segregation already during my childhood years – before 1950.

It is hard to believe that the church played such a leading role in the discrimination of the non-white people. One may try to understand these actions against people of other faith, but many colored people became members of the Dutch Reformed and so-called "sister" churches, yet those people were always treated as non-whites or secondary citizens.

Members of the white congregation were conducting Sunday afternoon services at the colored congregation for free, but the colored people never attended a service of a white congregation – maybe during a funeral service. There was never any real effort made to bring the different nations and cultures together.

That is one concept that has never made sense to me. Surely God's people are defined by their unity of faith and not by their color or background?

Segregation was a convenient way to protect what our leaders wanted to protect and other considerations were secondary.

Many missionaries were supported who preached in other parts of Africa. The goal of the church was to try and save souls and leave the well being of the physical man up to himself and the civil authorities. The soul was valued as good enough for God's message, but definitely not as part of His white congregation.

The concept of not mixing church and state was never applied. The civil leaders were strongly influenced by the viewpoint of church leaders and there was therefore never any real difference of opinion between church and civil leaders.

I guess that that many politicians had two reasons why they so strongly supported this church philosophy. Many of them grew up having been taught this doctrine and for that reason, they firmly believed that it was right in the sight of God.

Then there was also the job-security motivation. A politician knows that his job is to keep the voters happy. There were no voters other than the white people and most of them were Dutch Reformers anyway. So it was a logical policy to follow.

There were a few "extremists" like Beyers Naude who dared to question the right and wrong of these policies. He spent many nights in jail for so-called "questioning". We all thought this man was way out of line because we were too ignorant and brainwashed to think for ourselves.

This situation carried on like that for many years. There were many of us who found difficulty in understanding what was necessary to stop the outside world's criticism. To us people like Nelson Mandela and other ANC members were heathen and terrorists.

CHAPTER 5.

THE PEOPLE WE MET DAILY

We lived in a society of predominantly white people. There were a few colored families living in the area and they were all working as gardeners or house cleaners for the white people. I never understood that really as a child, and really did not have much time to worry about it either. I attended the only primary school in the immediate area and only white children went there. We always believed that there was a school for colored children a few miles away, but I never saw it. Most of the colored children living in Olifantshoek never went to school as far as I could tell. The colored people called the whites "baas" and "mies" which was like "boss" and "madam". We in turn called the men "outa" which was a respectful "old man" or the women "aia" which is a word for an adult woman. First names were very seldom used and were always preceded by one of these adjectives.

Address forms such as these disappeared greatly in South Africa later on in years and were replaced with words such as "master" or "madam". There are those however, white and colored, who grew up with it that probably still use it today.

Some of them were big friends of ours. We played games together and hunted (mostly birds) together. Although they acted in a subjective way, they were never slaves. They had freedom to come and go as they please. The only relationship they had with the white people was that of employer and employee. This was not a concept developed in South Africa. Jan van Riebeeck arrived in Cape Town from Holland with "chamber maids". The servant concept was also applied in Biblical times, but it we never bought or traded any person.

Our lives were about surviving as poor people and yes, we recognized that there were others even poorer and less fortunate than ourselves. We treated those people with the same respect as we did those who were more privileged, although we had less admiration for them.

I had my own vegetable garden. Although I was not even a teenager yet, I often had to help my dad in cultivating the fields where we grew sweet potatoes, potatoes, pumpkin and various other vegetables.

So, I got my own piece of garden to plant and sold all the produce to the colored people. They were eager to buy from me because my products were fresh out of the garden and inexpensive. We were not taught to be greedy and rip other people off and so we had no reason to feel guilty about any trading deal.

We lived in an area where there were no black ethnic groups. The only times we ever saw black people, when we saw groups of men working on the roads. These were people who helped with the upkeep of the gravel roads.

They did not speak our language. They appeared very unfriendly and we were scared of them. We could not communicate with them and we did not trust them. In fact, there was never any opportunity to build any kind of friendship or trusting relationship.

They must have seen us as occupants of their country and would not have understood our side of the story. Our culture was very different to theirs and so there was no common bond or interest anywhere.

They had their own beliefs and practices. No churches and only witchdoctors. It took many years before any of them were ever converted to our faith and beliefs, but even those remained different in their own cultures and outlook on life. We had a Western, capitalistic culture and this was foreign to Africa. We believed in a one-woman-one-man marriage relationship, but in Africa a man's wealth was often counted in the number of wives he possessed. Young ladies were traded by their fathers for a dowry (normally a number of cattle) to a husband she may never have loved – something completely unheard of in our custom. The women were in subjection to the men and even if a man would mistreat his wife, she would not dare to leave him as this would bring reproach on her family.

We believed that the black people had very little respect for human life. This scary thought became more real when TV came to South Africa and we had the opportunity to witness some of the cruelties that they would inflict upon one another. What is even worse is the fact that the news media often helped to incite these actions. Young children enjoyed the media attention and would go to the extreme to get the cameras focused on them.

It sounds cruel to describe the culture amongst the black people in Africa in a derogative way, but one needs to have lived there to understand some of these perceptions. There are numerous ethnic groups of which the Xhosa, Zulu, Sotho, Tswana, Venda and Ndebele were the biggest and most prominent groups. Many of these groups have always treated the others with some mistrust and groups like the Xhosas and Zulus have never lived in peace with one another. It was probably this division amongst them that gave the white people the opportunity to rule this land.

The arrival of the white man with a different culture just added more oil to a proverbial fire.

This difference in language, culture and faith has remained the biggest obstacle in the human race even up to today. We do not often read of conflicts between nations where these three practices are shared. However, the world has been at war just about non-stop between nations of different cultures. We all wanted everyone else to see and understand things our way and, while we try and persuade one another, our cultures are so engraved in our hearts and minds that true conversion into another culture is a very scarce and unique occurrence. One nation's values or intentions may never be understood by another.

It was later in my school career that I learned more of the struggles between white and black. Sure, I learned the white man's viewpoint and history as written by the white man, but even today I still do not find it all that strange. Whenever there are opposite parties involved in life situation, there will always be two sides of the same story told. Only an unbiased judge could really evaluate the evidence and make a righteous judgment. Unfortunately, unbiased judges are very hard to find – anywhere.

I learned about the difference in cultures. I learned about wars and struggles for land and power. I learned very little about political viewpoints. In fact, we basically accepted only one political viewpoint; namely "survival".

So in South Africa, it was always either the black people or the white people. There was never a nation under one flag or under one God. We believed that if the black people would rule, it would mean the end of the whites.

We shared a country with approximately 15 ethnic groups and each one of them wanted to rule everyone else.

CHAPTER 6.

PERCEPTIONS OR FACTS

Were the black ethnic groups really our enemies? What would they do if they were in control of the country? Would they recognize minority rights? What standard of judgment would they use?

These questions were real questions and no white government was prepared to let down their guard to find out. These answers were also not guided by moral or religious values, but by cold, hard facts as it were experienced on a daily basis.

The white people knew they were foreigners in this land and unwanted. We felt that the black people hated us because of that and that they viewed us as enemies. By the time I was born, we felt this land was ours as much as anyone else's and we were prepared to defend our heritage with everything at our disposal.

The second question is not difficult to answer either. Africa provided the answer for us and we clearly understood that no leader in Africa shared power. Democracy was a Western dream and completely unacceptable by most African countries. Once a black ethnic group gets the power, the rest of the people become puppets and are lucky if they have any means of self-enhancement.

So the next question is already answered. Minorities have little or no rights in Africa at all. In many countries, farm animals have better lives. Mankind as a whole has learned many values as communication developed and civilization spread, yet tolerance and protection of minority rights, are even in the most advanced countries still questionable. So, in third world countries with limited appreciation for civilization, like in Africa, only a fool will bet on any right whatsoever.

The barrel of the gun has always been the only standard of judgment. Very few of these ethnic groups knew of or have heard of the compassion of one nation for another. Their judgments were based on tribal cultures and practices and most likely do not consider things like constitutions or individual rights. They are influenced by witchdoctors and faith in dead spirits. These beliefs were very foreign to us and to be honest, we believed that those were the reasons why there was no hope of a practical, peaceful society.

So the answer was an African one. Do what you can to survive – and the white man had the intelligence to do just that. This fact was probably the reason why the white man was seen as a racist and monster.

The settlers brought with them technical knowledge and education. They had various trades and skills. They were not scared of work and while the black ethnic men were sitting smoking their pipes and the woman were tilling the fields, the white families worked their hands to the bone to provide for their own. They planted their fields and applied strong agricultural practices to get the maximum out of the ground and from their livestock. There was great co-operation amongst the community and this unity was their strength. This led to their prosperity and jealousy from their neighbors.

So, jealousy brings hatred. The more the white people prospered, the greater the jealousy and hatred grew. Prosperity also brought with it power. This is a fact of life that is applied in every society; never mind how democratic such a society is. Money is used to persuade and to enforce and to inform. The media is bought and will justify the standpoint of their owners and shareholders even if such a standpoint was rotten as hell itself.

Unfortunately, the white man's power also contained elements of corruption and misuse. Mankind seems to be without resistance against his personal greed when put in a position of power. The old cliché that "power corrupts" has been proven over and over.

So survival in Southern Africa was like a major chess game. Every move by your opponent must be answered by a counter move. It was a matter of keeping the noose tight so that you can keep the advantage and deny your opponent the opportunity to overpower you. Some of the strategies followed were very much against the religious teachings of "loving thy neighbor", but it is ironic what one would be prepared to give up for survival.

The saddest of all is that at least two generations of white South Africans grew up with this inner conflict of misguided church teachings and the ever-conscious fear of being overpowered by another culture. Fortunately, today's generation have realized the mistakes of the past and have taken bold steps to help and rectify these wrongs. Hopefully, those fears of the past were misguided but only time will tell.

Is it only the white South Africans that have made such great and cruel mistakes? Maybe one should be a little more objective and consider the current world situation. My own participation in the apartheid life style and reflecting upon it, forces me to look around me and evaluate life as I witness it today.

So I consider the current state of worldwide morality today compared to that of 50 years ago. What has that got to do with apartheid? To some such a comparison is ridiculous. However, the so-called "baby-boomers" can all testify that they neglected to teach their children the same good quality principles that their parents taught them. They robbed their own children of the most valuable qualities of life. They robbed their families of the very principles of "families" and they have created a generation governed by greed and filth. We have all inherited a society where everything is about me.

That has all been done under the banner of "rights" and "freedom". What a mockery! There is no freedom for a child who does not know in which house he or she really belongs. There is no freedom for a child who is forced by society to become the competition tools of parents and coaches. Children reach out to drugs because they are looking for some sort of security and drugs may ease their anxiety. Their role models are not spiritual parents and teachers anymore, but celebrities who are just as insecure and without direction themselves.

Yes, there are some of these children who will become famous and probably even rich. That is today's standard for success. The character that was lost in the process and the monster that was created does not matter. Apparently, this is what a "right" is.

Therefore, just as so many were concerned for the mistreated South African blacks and rightfully so, there are still sane people concerned for this generation. The mistreatment may not appear to be so similarly cruel, but the final outcome may be dramatically worse.

I am very grateful that the white government in South Africa realized the errors of apartheid and gave democracy a fair chance. I just hope and pray that someone has enough sense and wisdom to address the decay of mankind and that bold steps can be taken before mankind destroyed himself completely.

CHAPTER 7.

WHITE SOUTH AFRICAN POLITICS

There were two main political parties during most of my childhood years, namely the ruling National Party and the opposition United Party. Many years later parties like the Progressive and Democratic Alliance appeared on the scene. While some of the opposing parties may have had visions of a free open society, their message was never strong enough to get the attention from the average South African white voter.

The white Nationalist governments used the church teachings effectively in indoctrinating the white voters even further. They used these religious beliefs and real-life concerns to establish a system to protect the white people. The white voters did not have any better answers or solutions and did not consider how unfair our lifestyles became. No one focused on any corruption or any fraudulent practices. None of us really knew about such possibilities while I was growing up and to say the least, we did not really care. Life was way too tough and the news media was not something we studied on a daily basis. In fact, the media did not have the freedom to expose federal misdoings as much as they wanted to anyway.

So we grew up hearing about sanctions and we could not understand it. We understood what the world wanted, but we knew that to satisfy the world was to abdicate and wait for our own destruction. We believed that "separate development" had a slight possibility of succeeding. The idea was to have homelands where each nation could take care of their own without the difficulties of a mixed society.

This concept appeared reasonable. The different ethnic groups were already separated when the white people arrived in the country. It was not a mixed society, but rather different nations sharing the same land proportionately and sometimes separated by miles of unoccupied land, rivers or mountains. The presence of the white settlers resulted in the building of transportations routes that never existed before. The country developed from a third world nation to a country with a modern infrastructure and up-to-date technologies.

Unfortunately, this seemingly fair concept developed into the ugly word "apartheid". Apartheid originated due to the difficulties of enforcing the "homeland" concept.
Homelands were assigned based on the portions of the country where the individual ethnic black groups traditionally lived.

Apartheid was established through a number of very unreasonable and discriminatory laws. South Africans basically lived an apartheid life style while the country was still under British rule. It was however, after the National Party won the election in 1948, that some of these everyday practices were put on the law books and advertised the system to the world.

The most unreasonable of these laws was the "group areas act" supported by the "passbook" law. The group areas act legalized the homeland concept and also prohibited the purchasing of land by non-whites amongst the white communities. What made the homeland concept very unpopular was that many of these black people never lived in the actual homeland but in cities which fell under the white rule. The homeland concept was rejected by most black people, but the federal government enforced it nevertheless. The third law that supported this separate development was the "mixed marriage act" that stipulated that white people were not allowed to date or to marry non-whites.

The passbook law dictated that the black ethnic groups were forced to carry a passbook outside of their homelands similar to a passport, while the white, colored and other non-black groups had freedom of movement without such controls except when entering one of the homelands. The individual homelands were therefore treated as foreign states without the actual agreement from the black ethnic groups.

None of the major cities or harbors fell within the boundaries of these homelands and it is therefore easy to understand why the black groups opposed the idea. The government wanted to keep federal control over the infrastructure of the country because it viewed itself as the guardians of the progress in a land shared by 1st as well as 3rd world nations.

The idea was to limit black people to flock to the cities looking for work while there was no accommodation for them. It was also intended to avoid squatting townships from developing.

The country was rich with natural resources with many job opportunities but, unfortunately, these resources were not evenly divided amongst the relevant homelands. The result was the need for many migration workers that resulted in the splitting up of families. Laborers in the mining industry were mostly from the black ethnic groups and these nations suffered greatly. Black families were caught between the lack of job opportunities near their homes and the lack of infrastructure to accommodate families in the mining fields.

Laborers were housed in dormitories and the men had to leave their wives and kids in the homelands and were separated from them for months at a time. This situation led to the breaking up of family discipline and encouraged adultery. This again resulted in the spreading of sexual diseases.

These laws caused great displeasure and animosity in the country. The white people used their education to their own financial success and this brought about further jealousy and hatred. The government was accused of giving beautiful homes to the whites while the blacks had to live in huts and shacks. This was not true. These same successful white people paid the taxes in the country that made it possible for the authorities to build the infrastructure in the country that benefited all the occupants of the land.

So after 50 years of "apartheid" rule, the white South African government again confirmed what we all already knew – politics is about power and power corrupts. We saw the dangers of a state where the church had too much influence just like we see in countries where the Islamic leaders control their governments.

So those that proclaim separation of state and church find something to be satisfied about. However, before we get carried away with a slam-dunk case, the separation of church and state may even have worse results. The consequences of such an arrangement can be witnessed in many Western governments. The government is not held accountable by any moral society and therefore morality is lost and so the society is drowned in immoral filth.

Governments believe that they only have to abide by the law of the land. Again, these laws never touch on anything spiritual and therefore the physical adherence of what is written in the law is all that matters to them. Further judgments are made by lawyers and judges who again, have no spiritual obligation. To add fuel to the fire, they find it within their own interests to use the physical law in preference to spiritual reasoning, because they are not bound by any moral standards.

I will never forget a presentation that I attended given by a member of the South African Secret Agency in the early 1980's. His message basically was that if communism wanted to conquer any country, the financial or military options are not considered because of the risk and expense. He went on to say that the right strategy would be to break down the moral values and after that, a take-over becomes so much easier.

So the moral standards of the society become the responsibility of families and churches. The family unit could not withstand the onslaught of the media without conscience and an entertainment world that thrives on the most despicable forms of promiscuity. Broken homes have become a standard in society, and mothers and fathers are so busy trying to chase after these phantoms of what fall under the labels of "success", that children are left with scraps or leftovers of the real values of life.

Then we stand amazed when children become drug addicts or babies are born to young kids.

Many churches have become fronts for wolves in sheep clothing. Just like in South Africa, many members are brainwashed and many church coffers are filled with contributions of those with non-spiritual agendas. It is common today to find individuals who use a form of religious connotation to promote their own political or commercial goals.

So the South African politics were also infiltrated by phenomena that we describe as "power and status". The idea of "survival of the fittest" is not an evolutionary concept, but engraved in man's everyday motivations. The lengths mankind will go to are only limited by opportunities and resistance from others.

CHAPTER 8.

CONTROL VERSUS FREEDOM

I have had the pleasure (or displeasure) in my fifty-odd years to experience systems of federal control and that of so-called freedom.

I say so-called freedom, because "freedom" is a relative phrase. I think that I felt freer under reasonably strict control than where it did not exist.

Let me try and explain. Although I was one of the supposedly privileged white South Africans, I lived in an era where there were many limitations. South Africa had computers long before we had television. I helped to implement banking computer systems in 1971 but television came to the country only in 1975. We only had three channels and those were managed by the South African Broadcasting Corporation, a semi-government institution. The result was that the media coverage in the country was limited compared with more advanced countries. In addition, any liberality in news reporting was looked at with suspicion and often thought of as unpatriotic. We did not have any discussion program that could help us understand another viewpoint. We only had the limited message which we became accustomed to. It did not bother me, because I was trying to make the best of my little life and left the worries to those who wanted to rule the world.

Yet, this limited access to the bad news of my own country and the problems of the world, created a sense of false security and minimized my own concerns with everything else. No, that is not right, but that was my little world and I felt "free" in it. As far as I was concerned, those in authority were in control, I could do nothing about nothing, and as long as I personally do not transgress the law of the land, I could live my life in peace and harmony.

The laws that aimed at separation of nations and cultures did not affect me at all. I lived amongst my own people, I hated no one, and I was never forced into or out of relationships that I personally valued.

So I was free.

Nobody threatened my religion. The community dictated what was acceptable or not – and that applied to both school and church. We had no race issues in our community because we all were born into this life-style and we tried to keep the status quo. The school was under a federal government with strong religious affiliations and there were never debates about prayer or not on school property.

So even in a separate society, we had harmony. We did not view the financial advantage of one family over another as discrimination, but rather as fortitude and the proof of education versus the lack of it. That helped to encourage each young white generation to pursue careers that would provide these benefits.

Why did the black and colored people not do the same? Part of it was definitely the government's fault. It was surely so, because white children were forced to get an education while nobody applied any pressure on black families. There were exceptions. Willie (a colored man who worked for the local butcher) made sure that his children went to school to get education.

We all loved and respected this man. Now, if he could, why not the other colored or black families? Was it perhaps that they were working harder at politics, just like some today, instead of at guiding their families? Was it perhaps that they believed just like I, that they could not do anything about the situation in the country and just gave up? I don't have the true answer, but sometimes we can do a lot about our own destinies.

There were other controls that we had to accept. TV programs were strictly censored against any form of profanity, immorality and the like. Programs were aimed at the family and those who were looking for a more liberal form of entertainment, would not have found it on national television. We were not even aware of these restrictions as none of us were interested in that type of entertainment in any case.

Pornography in any form or fashion was prohibited. Those found guilty of such possession, were fined and such material confiscated.

In today's society, that supposedly was taking away of our rights.

They took away our rights to be an unholy and ungodly generation. Living a life of freedom to me is like enjoying the sunshine. When we enjoy it responsibly, it is good and pleasant. However, when we become careless and get over-exposed, we can get burned. So we require some sort of protection. Spiritual and moral laws are just as necessary for a society as the law of the land.

Yes, we also had freedom from all this filth that stares us in the eyes on a daily basis. We had freedom to respect each other. Parents had freedom to discipline their children and children had freedom to expect quality guidance from their parents. Children even had freedom to expect mother and father both at home for suppertime.

Divorce cases were an abomination and adulterers and fornicators were noted by society. Although many of these principles came from the religious background, even those who had no religious interest valued these principles.

So we were living in a country that had many governmental controls. Theoretically, we should have been very unhappy people. Yet, comparing it to the standards of the western world in the 21st century, our lack of rights and freedoms was our greatest blessing. We are capable of making a comparison based on real-life experiences and the answer is simple: Freedom isn't free if you have no protection from the evils of the lusts of this world. Yes, if the only standard we live by is our own opinion and federal laws, we will be enslaved by greed and other physical demands and the less ambitious and less talented will be dominated anyway.

CHAPTER 9.

THE WORK ENVIRONMENT

In 1968 I discovered some of the more dramatic impacts of apartheid. I graduated from high school in 1967 and because we had no means for me to attend university, I took a job with the Deeds Office in Cape Town. This was my first experience of city life and I quickly realized what a protective and innocent life I have been living up till then.

I obviously had no transport of my own and had to make use of public transportation to work as well as to the naval base where I was going to do my compulsory military training. The signs of "whites only" or "non-whites" only on trains and buses and other public facilities were an eye-opener. There was not much difference in the quality of the facilities between white and non-white, but the separation was very obvious.

I worked for banking corporations for most of my working career in South Africa. During a period of approximately 22 years in the Bancorp group, I only really had interaction with 3 non-white gentlemen, namely Alfred, Maxwell and Pikkie. Both Alfred and Maxwell were from the Zulu tribe while Pikkie was a colored Malayan Muslim.

These men did not have very high education, yet Maxwell did reach the position of manager in the division he worked. He was very proud of that achievement and we were happy for him. He was also an official in one of the black soccer teams and was obviously highly regarded by his fellow countrymen.

During an evening where we both received awards for long service in the bank, my wife and I sat at table with Maxwell and his wife. They did not at all show any discomforts during an evening of pomp and ceremony. So I thought: here is another example of a black man who overcame the difficulties of society and because he had his own aspirations, at least achieved some of them. This event also gave us the opportunity to share a social event with those of another color and culture and we were thankful for it.

Alfred was the mailman for our division and although he had very little education, was treated by everyone with kindness and respect for his age.

Pikkie was in charge of the office coffee and tea facilities as well as the mail (1972 – 1977) and was a friend of all of us. My boss and he often took bets on the weekly rugby outcomes and one of them always collected a packet of cigarettes from the other on Monday mornings.

There were other non-white people working for the bank, some as security guards or parking attendants, but very few achieved really any sort of senior or status position. The lack of formal education surely contributed to this. Later on in years I met some who were involved with computer and business systems development. These people were treated as equals by the management and their colleagues and one could sense that it was only a matter of time for the whites to share their work environment with other races on a more frequent and natural basis.

The black people worked mainly in the mining and industrial industries while colored people worked as farm laborers or house aids. There were not many non-white entrepreneurs and these people were very dependent on the whites for the growth and provisions of the country. The lack of specialized education obviously had a lot to do with it and in addition, the lack of financial resources or access to it, made it very difficult for any of them to become business owners. In contrast, the Indian community that lived in the country was great retailers and business owners and they seemed to achieve this by helping one another.

The number of educated non-white South Africans eventually grew and by the time we moved from Cape Town to Johannesburg in 1977, the universities of Witwatersrand, Natal and Cape Town had many black students.

CHAPTER 10.

SOUTH AFRICAN MILITARY

The white South Africans were responsible for the terrible system of apartheid. That was however not the only thing they were responsible for.

They were also responsible for the security of the country.

I grew up in an era when the whole world was in turmoil because of communism and the threat that it brought to every society. Two of the neighboring countries, Angola and Mozambique, had communistic tendencies and that increased the threat to the successful capitalistic white people of South Africa. These countries were once colonies of Portugal and the advancement in infrastructure was because of this colonialism.

I served 11 months in the South African navy as part of compulsory military service that each white young man had to participate in. Following those 11 months, I also had to attend monthly parades for a further 10 years.

During my service in the armed forces, I only know of one minesweeper manned by colored men. The rest of the armed forces were all white. So apartheid was not only applied to benefit the whites, but the system forced the white people to take total responsibility of the country and even the protection of the total population.

The South African armed forces fought side by side with the Allied forces in both World Wars. The Germans were defeated in South West Africa that later became Namibia. During the Peace of Versailles in 1919, this country was given to the South African government to administer. The United Nations criticized and questioned the South African rights to this administration for many years and this seemingly double standards aggravated the white people greatly. We were good enough to risk and give our lives during the wars, but everything South Africa did, was wrong because of apartheid.

The South African forces also assisted Jonah Savimbi in fighting the communists in Angola in the early eighties. The communists, strongly supported by Cuba with military assistance, would have taken over the total of the southern tip of Africa but for the resistance from a small white population of merely 5million. Many of the African and South African leaders were bed-partners with the Russians and Cubans and one could only imagine what could have happened. The end of the cold war, thanks to the hard work of men like Ronald Reagan , had little impact on the attitude and lifestyles of the Cubans and some of the African nations.

Many African nations found this action of the South African army as interference in other nation's affairs. Unfortunately, any action by the South African government was treated with suspicion because of the white government's internal policies. The communists were favorites in many neighboring countries and anything that came from South Africa was unwelcome.

CHAPTER 11.

SOUTH AFRICAN POLICE

The South African police force is no different from any other responsible law enforcement agency anywhere else in the world.

The police was often accused of this, that and the other. However, like the old saying goes: "if you want to hit a dog, you can easily find a stick". My uncle and some of my cousins joint the police force and I find it hard to believe that their intentions were anything different but to keep the law. These men and many of their colleagues grew up with the same teachings and principles that my parents taught me.

Yes, there are always those that will bring the force into bad repute, but those were the exceptions and very far from the rule. These cases disappointed all of us who were proud of our men in uniform. These law officers were often taunted and spat upon by those who knew the media cameras were there waiting on them to lose their patience and self-control.

Even those black people who wanted to see the law applied and were friendly to the police, found them at the short end of the stick. We have witnessed black people set alight with a gasoline-covered tire around their necks by their own people. Such acts were the cruelest that any person can perform on another and there was little the police could do to stop it. What is even worst is the fact that the media were there to film this and found it newsworthy instead trying to save the person being tortured. It has always amazes me how quickly those that do not want to get involved to assist someone else, can have so much to say. Another old saying comes to mind: "The best coach is sitting on the stands".

The police were often accused of mistreating prisoners. This is such an old, stale story. Everyone knows that prisoners get treated in many unkind ways in every prison in every country. Some get treated worse than others and the prisoner often has a great share in the treatment he receives. South African prisons are no different.

The South African police force was trained at formal colleges and was employed to ensure that the laws of the land were adhered to. Many policemen may have disagreed with some of the policies, yet they swore to uphold the law and fulfill their duties.

The activities of the South African Secret Police were just that: secret. The man in the street knew little of the operation of this task force unless you were someone of interest and had reason to be interrogated by them. Whether they actually did wire-tapping or used extreme interrogation methods, I do not know. There were many rumors of such.

CHAPTER 12.

THE NEW SOUTH AFRICA

The year 1992 was a great year in the South African history.

The Nationalist government under President F.W. de Klerk finally had enough conviction and courage to tackle the South African problem. So a referendum was held and 68% of the white voters agreed that it was time for a democratic and just political system in the country.

Did sanctions bring that about? I am not so sure. Sanctions often hurt those that it is supposed to help. There were many ways round the sanctions. When countries like the USA withdrew from South Africa, the Japanese, French and Germans quickly filled those vacant market spots. Instead of the GM products, South Africans bought Toyotas, VW's and BMW's.

Yes, sanctions may have helped, but not nearly as much as what it was supposed to have done. South Africa was under the rule of the Nationalist Party for 54 years before this dramatic change came about. The sanctions may have helped a great deal in forcing the internal development of South African technological abilities. SASOL, the South

African coal and oil mining giant, was a world leader in producing petrol or gasoline from coal in a reasonably cost-effective manner. Medical doctors and dentists could compete with the best in the world. Unfortunately, many of those doctors and dentists have by now left the country and have been replaced by Cubans with a lot less skills.

The courage of a man like Mr. De Klerk has never been proclaimed. He could have followed in the footsteps of his predecessors and followed the status quo. He could not have foreseen the outcome of the referendum and instead of a major political achievement could have faced the end of his political career.

I sincerely believe that the political changes that took place were because of the spiritual convictions men like F.W. de Klerk had. The world pressure surely helped. He, like many others, did some soul-searching and recognized the wrongful situation.

So he led the white people to a soul-searching decision and eventually the other inhabitants to democratic freedom. He let Nelson Mandela out of jail.

Mr. Nelson Mandela turned out to be a great statesman. I mentioned before that many of us believed he was just a terrorist, but having realized the truth of the South African situation, it is not difficult to understand the anger and hatred that men like him must have felt.

I would probably have felt the same, but I am not sure that I could have displayed the same dignified attitude as what he has done since his release from jail.

Mr. Mandela's release, free elections for every one and no more apartheid laws, all were aiming at bringing about a better South Africa. Even some of the teachings of the Dutch Reform church were adapted to facilitate the "new South Africa". Although, I must add, there are still many of the staunch believers that would still defend and try and justify the old system.

South Africa is currently (2006) experiencing a booming period. Great developments have taken place and many black people have become very rich, very quickly. Affirmative action has allowed black people to find good jobs and earn good money. This newly found prosperity is visible by the new Mercedes Benz, Audi and BMW cars driven by black people.

While one is holding thumbs that this prosperity will continue, there are already signs that some of the affirmative action may be counter-productive. Interference by the government in the agricultural section and the forcing of black people in the farming business may eventually kill the goose that lays the golden eggs. Farming in South Africa is highly scientific and while there may be a great desire for the black people to share in this very successful business, the country as a whole cannot afford any slowing down of production. It will be years before the agricultural achievements by the current farmers will be emulated by any one in the black community. Zimbabwe tried that affirmative action and the results are known as catastrophically.

Another dark cloud on the horizon is that the newly found riches are limited to a small percentage of the non-white community. There is therefore still a large part of the community who live in poverty and that is always a motivation for unrest.

61

Then there are many stories of corruption amongst governmental departments and the misuse of power.

I have spoken to many people who feel that Mr. Nelson Mandela is the stabilizing factor in the current situation. They believe that once he is gone, a more extreme group will start pushing for their own agenda.

In the mean time, my family and I have set our own goals and objectives for our future. We have two daughters and a son and the thought of raising our children in this very insecure environment was very nerve wrecking. Our house was broken in twice within two years. The burglar bars and alarm system did not help. We lost valuable and sentimental possessions. Two of our automobiles were also stolen while living in Johannesburg.

So, what do we do? We could not move elsewhere inside the country, as I was settled in my job and there were no chances of a transfer or finding something similar in a safer location.

We finally made a decision similar to what our forefathers made centuries ago. No, we were not going to run away, we just decided to explore our options for the benefit of our children. Fortunately, we were going to a country with cultures and religion similar to ours and so we were hoping to find like-minded people that will welcome us.

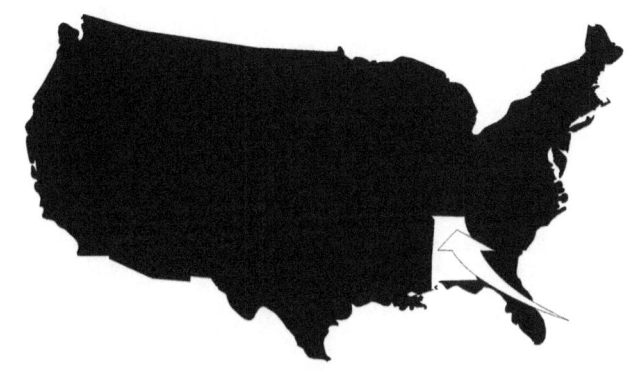

PART 2

MOVING TO AMERICA

CHAPTER 1.

THE EARLY YEARS

It all started in 1973, the year in which we were married.

It was about a month before our wedding date when we were introduced to Alan Fraser, and the truth of the gospel. After many evenings of Bible study, five of us obeyed the gospel and were baptized on one night - Karen, her mom, her sister Olivia, Olivia's husband Frans, and I.

There were no extra-ordinary experiences or special spiritual insights. We were only faced with the "black and white" facts of the Gospel, and all it took was honesty and obedience.

So we responded and that made us happy. Very happy!

All of this took place in Chantecler near Cape Town, South Africa. This was the beginning of what eventually would turn out to be a life of experiences, faith, drama and anxiety.

We were so excited initially, because we were going to convert the world for Christ. We learned to read God's Word, the Bible, with the intent of "seek and you shall find" and discovered that the total of God's will for mankind was contained within those pages. All we needed to do was to humble ourselves and to be honest and obedient.

Our wedding date was only a week later - August 25, so we had more than one reason to be excited. We were excited because we found the truth of the gospel, and also an immediate bond on which to base our married life. We knew that as I previously was a member of the Dutch Reformed Church and Karen a member of the Church of England, it potentially could put unnecessary pressure on our relationship. I have always believed that a man and wife should be of the same mind and judgment, especially in serious matters like religion, in order to make a marriage work and God knew how much that meant to us.

Alan was the instigator with this American idea.

This big redheaded, dynamic preacher inspired us with his zeal and enthusiasm for the gospel. His stories of his experiences while studying at Freed Hardeman College in Henderson, Tennessee, where he prepared himself as a preacher of the gospel, captivated us.

My enthusiasm for these newly found truths and my persistence in getting him to help me learn more each day, gave him the idea that maybe I should follow in his steps and become a gospel preacher as well.

He challenged and inspired me at every opportunity, and his motivation had the necessary influence on me. I remembered what one of my school friends in high school once told me. "You are going to be a preacher". I do not know where he got the idea from, but somehow it started making sense.

I often had that desire, although my faith was just not strong enough so early in my Christian life. Although I did not become a preacher, I have always had this need inside of me to be fruitful in the Kingdom - the kingdom of heaven - the one that Christ died for.

What a tremendous opportunity we have!

So I tried everything in the Church. I lead songs, prayers, and eventually got to teach and preach. I enjoyed it very much as it challenged me to study more and more. I never wanted to be accused of teaching false doctrine so finding the truth in God's Word was a major objective. I also loved the idea of presenting logical thoughts to the listeners.

The knowledge that the message of the Cross-was the best topic to be presented on earth inspired me more.

I never had official training except for a correspondence course on Timothy and Titus that Alan directed. I was therefore, untrained as far as the academics were concerned, but that did not bother me much. God used uneducated fisherman to spread His word in the first century and if He wanted me to do the same, I was ready.

I learned by trying to disprove everything I grew up with and eventually was able to distinguish between gospel truths, and human traditions. I learned from great gospel preachers and Bible scholars. I learned by watching these men giving themselves for their faith and for anyone who had time enough to listen.

First there was Alan. Alan impressed us with his dynamic nature and forceful preaching style.

Then came Eddie Bristow, a man that I loved like my own father. He was not as charismatic as Alan, but he impressed me with his strength and stability. He was a great Bible scholar and one of my greatest friends ever.

Then Norman Flynn came with his quiet and patient ways. A man whose wisdom left great imprints in our lives. We did not know it at the time but Norman was going to play a major role in our future.

Bob Pearce was another one. His great love for the gospel and his soft gentle nature made it a wonderful experience to be in his presence.

These men were great gifts from God to mankind, and especially to me. Each one of them carved great memories in my heart - some in the teachings of the gospel, others by their examples in being godly and God-fearing men.

Today I am wise enough to count these blessings that God so richly bestowed on me.

Oh, if only they knew how I appreciated every bid of time I spent with them!

I frustrated them often, because I was often very impulsive and sometimes hardheaded. However, that did not mean that I did not have many hours of gratitude for God allowing me to learn from their wisdom and knowledge.

I will never forget how I often interrupted Alan's busy programs by calling him at every possible opportunity while I was searching the Scriptures, and not being able to find all the answers for myself. One day, while on our way to watch the British Lions play one of our provincial rugby teams, Alan told me, "Today we are going to talk rugby. Not Bible."

I had to laugh as I realized that too much of a good thing might not even be good enough for a gospel preacher! I figured that it was fair to give him a break and I focused on rugby until the next time.

I loved each one of them so much. Eddy has gone to his eternal home. The others are still busy influencing the lives of other people for God and His kingdom's sake.

Alan got us really interested in going to America.

The initial idea of becoming a preacher stayed with me for a while but I soon realized that it was only an impulsive dream. As I worked with these men I often realized my shortcomings and envied their talents.

There were, however, many opportunities to be fruitful without being in the spotlight of the pulpit and I started understanding that. There were many opportunities even for the one-talented person. So I focused on some of those.

The idea of going to the States never vanished. It was always somewhere in the back of my mind. One day, maybe one day, we are going to have that chance.

As Christians, we lived our lives trying to do the right things, but we trusted God with our needs and even desires. So we prayed and asked God to open doors for us.

We were hoping God would respond quickly, but we had to be patient.

God works within His own timeframes.

CHAPTER 2.

THE FIRST TRIP OVERSEAS

As systems analyst and eventually project manager for Trust Bank in Johannesburg, South Africa, doors opened for me. I only realized years later that we have to be very patient when we ask God for anything.

Trust Bank bought computer systems from a software company in Dallas, Texas. We were really impressed with the philosophies of the Hogan systems, but these systems were designed for the American banking industry and required major customization for the South African banking environment.

A special project team was assigned to handle this customization and I was one of them.

I could not believe my luck!

Years later I examined all the events that took place following this assignment and came to the conclusion that there is no such thing as luck. I remembered Romans 8:28, "And we know that all things work together for good to those who love God..." and was amazed at my blindness.

Some people may still call it luck - or coincidence. Call it what you like. The apostle Paul knew exactly what he meant in that passage and I discovered it for myself. God blesses His people, and more often than not in multiples of what we are hoping for.

The project team was called "Bankorp Hogan Systems". Bankorp was the holding company. We were proud of being part of it all and were looking forward to the challenges, and all the limelight it was going to bring us. The project was definitely not an easy one and it was going to require the best of the best to deliver what was expected of us.

What I did not realize is that there was much more than just limelight to be enjoyed.

The project was started in June of 1985 and by September of that year I was one of four managers to be sent to Dallas on a training course. I finally had an opportunity, paid for by the company, to visit the great U.S. of America.

A trip was planned to America, land of opportunities, and the world leader in just about everything.

I, Christian Gerber, was going to there and see it for myself.

I wanted to take Karen with me, but I would have had to pay for her ticket and could most definitely not afford it.

By now we had three children - Natalie 7, Wayne 5 and Melissa 2. Mom Karen had to watch over them while Dad got to visit the land of Columbus and George Washington and of course, Elvis.

Wow!

The trip had everything in it that I hoped for.

Norman Flynn and his wife, Joyce, were working with the Central congregation of the Church of Christ in Gadsden, Alabama, and I had time to visit with them. The relationship we established while Norman was preaching for us in Florida, South Africa, grew over the years to something we would treasure for the rest of our lives. The Gerbers and Flynns became like real family. We were already blood related through Him who died for us, but as the years went on, my children started treating Norman and Joyce as grand parents and to us they were real family.

I did not realize at this time how much this friendship would still mean to us and benefit us in the years to come.

So I visited with Norman and Joyce in Gadsden. Brother Baker, an elder in the congregation, invited us for watermelon on his farm.

I saw how the Americans lived in the cities and in the country. I met with worldly as well as very spiritual people. We visited the Nocalula Falls and bought ice cream at Jack's.

I saw the real America all on my very first trip.

I said first, because I eventually made seven trips.

The watermelon was nice, and so was the company. I was given the biggest piece of watermelon and while trying to eat it, had questions fired at me about life in South Africa and about Karen and the kids. I enjoyed telling them, never realizing that while I was talking, they were eating their watermelon and I fell behind.

It didn't matter. I enjoyed my watermelon, and they were captivated by my stories.

The people in Dallas were very different. Some of them viewed us as people out of Africa - uneducated and used to wild animals roaming the streets. We enjoyed it - that was their ignorance. We were educated, and did not see wild animals other than in well established and managed game reserves.

One young man enjoyed showing us the Reunion building and elevators. He thought it was a great experience for the Africans and we pretended to be impressed.

All of our cities had modern buildings like that, but how was he to know?

Yes, we were out of Africa, but not everything out of Africa was third world. The trip was educational and interesting. We arrived home with lots of gifts and stories to tell.

Meanwhile, the idea of moving to America stuck its neck out again. This time there was a different reason.

The Hogan philosophies were unique in the development of application systems and experienced developers were hard to find. Being able to share the things I have learned during my years as a programmer and systems analyst with other people in the same field, became an exciting new challenge and I started looking for opportunities to achieve that.

I was still an active participant in church activities. My knowledge of scripture was now comparatively good, and our dedication to be good Christians helped us thought of through difficult years. The Church was relatively small in South Africa and being able to worship in congregations with more than fifty members was breathtaking, to say the least. We have only once or twice since 1973 worshipped with 500 or more people at any given time, and we enjoyed the wonderful fellowship and especially the singing.

Can you imagine being able to do that on a regular basis? The thought of it excited us so much that we could not see the wood from the trees and never thought of the price to pay to achieve that.

I started looking for employment opportunities in America. The fact that I was in management did not help my aspirations much. Companies were interested in programmer and analyst skills, and it was by now about 4 years since I did any hands-on development.

My promotions basically took me out of the market!

One company offered me a job as an analyst. I considered it, although it was a step down. The thought of moving to America was much greater than the management status. The job had one snag, however. It was for a contract worker with no definite location and security. Something inside of me did not like that and I brushed the idea aside.

I realized later that that was one of the best decisions I made in my life. We would have had a miserable life in trying to raise three children in a strange country with minimum finances.

Trips to the USA and Great Britain became a common thing over the next few years. I got promotion to senior manager and represented our company at Hogan user events, and made a presentation or two about our customization experiences.

By now the kids started attending school and we were pretty much a successful family.

In 1991 I had the first opportunity to take Karen with me on one of these trips. Many people would have jumped at such an opportunity, but not Karen. She was not easily going to go that far away from our children. Luckily my mother-in-law could afford the time to take care of the children while we were gone, and that seemed to put Karen's mind at ease.

Karen visited with Norman and Joyce, now living in Ider, Alabama, while I was doing my business. I managed to join Karen for three days before we had to return.

CHAPTER 3.

THE PRESSURE GETS WORSE

A third reason to move to America has by now become a major factor.

The political situation in South Africa may have appeared to the world at large as improving, as "apartheid" was about to be abolished, but to many South Africans, black and white, a traumatic era was dawning.

Abolishing apartheid was a great milestone in all of our lives, but in place of it came something that in years to come, may prove to be much worse.

Affirmative action gave birth to a society where mob-rule was at the order of the day, and murders, muggings, rapes and burglaries multiplied on a daily basis. We tried to protect our properties and possessions, which we worked so hard for, as best we could. There were burglar bars on windows, security gates on doors, alarm systems and watchdogs - all of these precautions to try and live a peaceful life.

None of these were of any good when you had to stop at a red traffic light and got mugged while stuck in the traffic and nobody with courage enough to help you.

This was the society and lifestyle that our children and their children were going to inherit.

We were never racists, nor politicians. We were victims of a system where hatred was nearly justified, and where evil was going to be revenged by more evil. We have always loved our country, but the thought of getting out of there for our children sake, became an obsession. Not being chicken, as some would call it, but being realistic and pro-active.

The only question we asked was: "How?"

In 1992 a catastrophe hit my business career. The Amalgamated Banks of South Africa (ABSA) took over Bankorp and its affiliates. Many senior people in the Bankorp group were demoted or had to find other jobs. I was one of the blessed ones to keep my position, but not without problems.

I started experiencing high blood pressure problems due to stress. I always thought I handled the take-over pretty good, but apparently not.

One of my colleagues asked me how I felt about the insecurity of the whole situation. I replied: "This one is too big for me. The Lord must take care of it."

Yes, I still trusted the Lord to take care of our affairs, but subconsciously I obviously still worried about it. The high blood pressure proofed it.

Our doctor was a homeopath and he took care of my stress problems with natural medication. My blood pressure dropped from 170/120 to 140/90 and we were quite satisfied with the results. In the meantime the job situation remained stressful as ABSA still had to cut back on excess management positions. My boss could not guarantee my job, as he was not in a position to guarantee his own.

I made another trip to the States that year. The trip was planned before the take-over, so they allowed us to continue with it. I tried every avenue to find a company that would offer me a job in the States.

No one was interested. My nineteen years in banking application development and seven years as a trained manager meant nothing. I was a foreigner and it was again a case of "who you know" instead of what you know.

I felt pretty rotten, especially when one of my colleagues who shared many of my trips overseas, announced that he was offered a job in Los Angeles and that he was taking it.

Surely the Lord could provide me with an opportunity as well!

It did not make much sense to me as I tried to get answers from God Almighty like Job of old. I probably would not have understood anyway if God had tried to explain to me. Maybe I thought that God owed me some!

How silly can one be?

Karen and I spoke about it often - and we prayed about it often. Somehow, some day God will give us that chance. We believed it.

We kept in touch with Norman and Joyce, hoping they may find something for us. Some South Africans participated in lottery draws to obtain green cards and were successful.

I was obstinate. If God will not provide an opportunity other than by luck, He is not willing for us to go. That thought seemed to allow me to apply some patience. I did not believe in a god that would want us to gamble for our future. He has too much control over our lives and I believed that if it was according to His will, everything would be achieved through practical and logical processes.

We believed that He could, but would He?

So we tried to be patient and planned a vacation trip to the United States for the family instead. However, the weakening of the South African rand against the dollar soon made us realize that we could not afford for all of us to go. After discussing it, we decided that I will take Natalie, now 15 and Wayne, 13 with me while Karen and Melissa will go and visit Karen's parents in Cape Town.

We met with a major stumbling block. We were due to leave on Friday, September 19, 1993 but Karen's mom phoned me at work on the Monday to tell me that Karen's dad had died.

It was a great shock although he was sick for a long time. Our plans were in jeopardy, but after careful consideration we decided that we still had a future ahead of us and that our children were our main priority.

We were going ahead with the trips as planned .The trip to the States was also intended to see how Natalie and Wayne would like the American lifestyle and environment, even if the trip was only for three weeks.

So we went ahead as planned. We were all very sad and upset, but we had to look ahead.

I felt terrible leaving Karen and her mom alone with their loss, yet we thought it through carefully and it was a decision we took together. I think we would probably have done the same if we had to make that decision again.

The trip to Orlando and to Ider, Alabama was a very memorable one for the three of us.

Natalie and Wayne quickly learned what traveling was all about. I got to know my two children and they got to understand a great deal about their dad. We spent five days in Orlando and twelve days with the Flynns. We had fun, but in the back of our minds were always the concern and longing for Karen and Melissa, knowing that they were experiencing the grief and sadness of an open grave.

This time Norman and I had a serious talk about our future.

Norman presented me with the jackpot solution. He told me about a program whereby foreigners may receive green cards to live in America.

They had to qualify as associate ministers, and an American congregation must be prepared to "adopt" them in that position. My twenty odd years in the church and everything I participated in, surely qualified me.

The only obstacle was to find a congregation willing to do that. Norman spoke to the congregation at Ider and they agreed to be our sponsor. All my trips to Ider and Karen's visit the previous year, finally paid off.

I knew that I still needed a full-time job, but that was another challenge for the Lord. Dorian Flynn, Norman's son, said to me one day, "Chris, come to the States - even if you have to come on faith alone."

I was reminded of that statement so many times afterwards. I often wondered afterwards whether I had enough faith for such a major step. Time had to tell, but we still had to apply and be accepted by the American government.

CHAPTER 4.

THE OPPORTUNITY ARRIVES

The Gerber family will remember the year 1994 for a very long time. This was a year of decisions, frustrations, anxiety and excitement. This was the year when I finally learned that counting your blessings should be done daily and not so every now and then. So I started counting and made notes of the very big ones.

Blessing Number 1.   Norman's dedication

Norman started pursuing the application for permanent residency on our behalf. This was no easy task and it was only then that I discovered how strongly he felt about us moving to America. He went through multiple efforts and letdowns in trying to find the right channels and federal departments before he finally managed to obtain the correct papers. He traveled more than once from Ider to Atlanta, Georgia, a three-hour trip. The program that we had to apply for, was not that well known, but Norman's persistence paid off.

Friends with this kind of dedication are very hard to find and we know God has and will bless him greatly for it.

Blessing Number 2.   The application papers arrive

It was still early in the year when the big envelope with all the application forms arrived. The American government required personal information on each one of the family members and detail of my experience in church work.

It was 21 years ago that Karen and I were baptized and started devoting our lives to the work of the Lord in leadership and support. We were founder members of the congregation in Kraaifontein, Cape Province, along with Eddy Bristow and one or two other families. We held many Bible studies and did just about anything possible to help the Church to grow in South Africa.

Yes, we believed we were as qualified as anyone else and just as devoted to this task as anyone else. So we completed those forms with utmost care and sent it with great anticipation to the immigration authorities in New York.

I promised the Lord that I would do whatever He required of me, if He made this move possible for us. I discovered a year later that it might not have been such a wise promise to make, as the Lord took me up on that.

Blessing Number 3.   The answer came

It was early June when we received the answer through the mail. The letter stated that we had been accepted, provided we can pass the final requirements as dictated by the American Consulate in South Africa. We were required to pass medical examinations, obtain tax and police clearance from the South African authorities and have a final interview with the consular in Johannesburg.

We were walking on clouds.

We were still not sure whether this meant green cards and were scared to ask, so we decided to wait for the interview before we made up our minds. The consulate informed us that the final interview could only be arranged once we had received the necessary clearance documents and our medical reports. So now we had to wait on outside parties to provide us with these papers.

The medical examination was no big deal and as we expected, everyone was in healthy, and the medical papers were prepared for us to present to the consular. Having achieved this first goal, seemed to motivate us while we were waiting for the police clearance forms.

Blessing Number 4.   Another trip

In the mean time, life carried on as usual in the business environment. We planned another one of those big, costly projects and another trip was arranged before the final steps were taken. Six of us had to travel to Dallas to evaluate our project plans with Hogan.

I decided that I needed that trip and would only inform my management about our plans after my return.

We had lots of fun as this was the first visit to the USA for more than one of the group, and their reaction to the American way of doing things was amusing to those of us who had experienced that before.

I discovered something on this trip that I have never noticed before - everything was not moonlight and roses in America.

I was strangely aware of all the risks of this large foreign country, and I thought of every possible thing that could possibly go wrong.

What if we do not earn enough money to supply in our basic needs? What if the kids do not fit into the environment? What if we have to live far away from our friends? What if we are forced to go back to South Africa and lose all the money we have invested in pursuit of this goal?

Continuous "what ifs".

After our return to South Africa, Karen found it hard to believe that I could become so negative overnight.

It took me a while, but one day the answer came to me out of nowhere. God is painting the total picture for me. He does not want us to make an important decision like this one with a blurred vision. We needed to see everything - the good, the bad and the possibly ugly. It was just like a father busy training his child.

"Keep your eyes open. Do not go through life with your eyes closed, because you may be fooled. Everything is not always what it seems. You have to consider both the good and the potentially bad before you make a great decision."

I thought of this and I said: "Wow! God, you are so real that it scares me!" But I was thankful and I needed every bit of that education before we took this big step.

I told Karen of my discovery and she agreed. She has always been one with great insight and spirituality. So we decided that if God will allow us to obtain the green cards, this move was according to His will. We told Him so in our prayers - just like Gideon and the dew on the fleece. Our expectations were not quite so vivid and radical as that of Gideon, but we still expected God to give us some direction in this decision.

Blessing Number 5.   The early appointment

It was middle August when, out of the blue, a letter from the American consulate arrived, informing us that our interview had been scheduled for Friday, September 2, 1994.

We were delighted, but shocked.

How could they go ahead with an interview while we were still waiting for our police clearance certificates, and were not really prepared? I called them and when the gentleman, who I spoke to, told me that they were doing us a favor, I did not understand. I concluded that our only choice was to try and see if we could speed up the process and get co-operation from the police headquarters in Pretoria.

I discovered later the importance of having the interview on that date, but that part of the episode must be told later.

They were right, they did us a big favor and we understood and appreciated it very much. The Lord was surely in control and He knew best. We decided that all we needed to do was to participate and He will see to the rest.

Blessing Number 6.   The police played game

I started inquiring about the whereabouts of our police clearance documents and the ladies at Florida police station helped me as much as what they could. However, even with all their assistance, I made no progress and the days were going by rapidly.

I finally decided that I had no choice but to take matters in my own hands and ventured out to the police headquarters in Pretoria - about 50 miles away. It didn't take me long to find the building and once I found the right floor and people to speak to, it only took me 5 minutes and I had all our documents in my hands. Again, everything came about so easy that it once again took me by surprise. I felt ashamed when I realized that my faith should have allowed me by now to see and understand God's will for us and to trust Him, instead of worrying unnecessary at times.

During all this time the question of whether we should go ahead with our plans, was still haunting us daily.

This decision could not be made on the spur of the moment and without rational and planmatic considerations. After all, we were going to lose a fair amount of hard-earned money, as this was a costly trip. In addition, the premature selling of our house and cashing in of some insurance policies would make us lose a great deal. We did not have much of a choice but to cash in as much as we could, in order to have the necessary funds for traveling and resettlement.

In addition, we were required to pay about R600 for the medical examination and R200 per person for our green card applications. Somehow the potential loss of money did not matter that much. We wanted a future for our children where we believed they would have a stable environment with the opportunities to further educate themselves, as well as being able to associate with fellow Christians as much as possible, and money was not nearly that important to us.

We were also concerned and two-minded about leaving our friends families and behind, and the thought of possibly never seeing some of them, made us very sad.

I attended a Kepner Tregoe course on decision analysis and applied some of this methodology to help us make a clear decision. This methodology included a "must objective" which focused on an absolute goal to achieve. The "must objective" in our situation was the stable future we had in mind for our children and we realized that if we were going to achieve that goal, everyone else would have to come second, even if it was going to make us sad.

Blessing Number 7.   My boss's reaction

The time had come for me to reveal my plans to my boss and our human resources department. These people held positions of authority which could have caused us major problems in achieving our goals, and I realized that the sooner I played open cards with them, the better my chances were for them to co-operate and possibly even assist us.

So I took the bull by the horns and made an appointment with Ken Boyd, my assistant general manager.

Ken's reaction to my news astonished me. He did not ask why or tried to dissuade me at all. In fact, when I told him that we had advanced plans to move to America, he replied: "I don't blame you. If I had the opportunity, I would probably do the same."

The rest of my interaction with him during that discussion, and in all the events following, was easy. I knew that he was not going to be a stumbling block. I decided then that I was going to play my part as best I could and I immediately started trying to identify a possible person to replace me in my job.

Although I was not one of the biggest experts in my field of Hogan lending systems, the unique experience I obtained by working with Hogan systems and the role the bank required me to play, limited the sources from whence I could draw such a replacement. I spoke to a young man who worked for me as a Hogan project manager, and within two weeks followed it up with an interview with him and Ken Boyd. He was offered the job, took it and I felt good having found my own replacement. I even had the opportunity to train him myself during the last month before our departure.

CHAPTER 5.

THE DAY OF THE INTERVIEW

B lessing Number 8.   The interview

Finally, Friday September 2, 1994 arrived - the day for our interview with the American consular. The whole family had to attend and by now I had all the documents available.

We arrived about 15 minutes early and there were already other families waiting. Everybody seemed so quiet and tense, knowing that this was the day our future was going to be determined for us by someone we have never met or spoken to in our lives.

God was going to use a stranger in our lives like He used Rahab, the harlot to assist the men from Israel.

I presented our forms to a gentleman behind the counter and after a while he asked me if I had any proof of our financial status, before we could continue. I had a letter in my briefcase stipulating the value of my pension fund, which was to be invested for us, and this seemed to suffice.

It felt like a lifetime before he finally invited us into a room where the consular sat waiting on us. The consular stayed in the adjacent room and spoke to us through a glass opening, possibly for security reasons. He was friendly and his questions were simple and precise:

Him: "What are you going to do in America?"
Me: "I am going to do whatever the Church wants me to do."
Him: "You are not going to be a full-time minister, is that correct?"
Me: "Yes, Sir."
Him: "Why Ider, Alabama?"

I explained about my business trips and our visits to Norman and Joyce. He was satisfied.

The questions started focusing on Karen and the kids. He even wanted to know if Melissa was married (she was 11 at the time). It broke the ice and we started relaxing a bit. He wanted to know when we planned to leave and I explained to him that we have still quite a number of issues to finalize in South Africa - we had to sell our house and the kids would only complete their school year in December. We would like to go in January 1995, if possible.

His next words hit my like a hammer.

"All of you have to be in America before the end of September 1994, because the program expires at the end of the month and if you do not get there in time, you will not be able to go," he said.

I thought Karen was going to cry.

His next sentence gave us hope again: "You are allowed to come back and finish your business, however."

It is then that things became clear for me and again I thought: "Wow, God, you are so fantastic!" Karen saw the smile on my face and I told her not to worry but that I will explain to her what it all means.

The consular concluded the discussion, told us to come and collect our documents in a week's time, and wished us well. Karen and the children were still perplexed, but Dad was smiling and rejoicing in his heart.

I explained to them on our way out: "Let us get to America, enter our documents, so we can get our green cards. The Lord has given us the time to come back and we will not be so pressed for time to finalize the issues in South Africa. I could not have come up with a better plan myself, knowing how long and frustrating the sale of a house could be."

The cost of an additional trip, my possibility of getting leave for a possible month or even two, and taking the children out of school for such a long period of time, did not worry me a bit. I rejoiced in my heart and thanked God for being such a wonderful Father.

Blessing Number 9.   Getting leave

Our division of the bank was enjoying a "spring day" at a nearby sports field that day and I could not get there soon enough to inform Ken about the results of the interview. Somehow I knew that he would understand and I was right. He told me to go ahead with my plans as I see fit and that he would support me as far as he could.

It could have been so much more difficult if someone else was in charge, but this time this assistant general manager had to respond to the instructions from the big Boss in the sky, although I don't think he knew that.

CHAPTER 6.

GETTING OUR GREEN CARDS

Blessing Number 10.   The critical trip

It was only when I got home that day that I realized the extent of the challenge ahead of us. We only had 28 days left in which to organize a trip for a family of five to the United States.

There were numerous questions to be answered. Where were we going to get R20, 000+ (about $6000 those days) for tickets plus spending money for an unknown period of time in such a short period of time? We were not exactly rich people and our savings account could not even cover half of that.

Where were we going to find a place to live for an unknown period of time that was both convenient and inexpensive? We knew that Norman and Joyce could possibly put us up for a week at the most, but we needed to find some other form of accommodation for the remainder of the period.

It was praying and serious praying, time again. This time however, we were fully aware of what the Lord has already achieved on our behalf and our prayers included a lot of "thank you".

Again, the answers fell into place as if someone was building a big puzzle. Both Karen and I had gold credit cards that we used on a very limited basis and we each had a R15000 credit limit. That could take care of any immediate expense that faced us.

We decided that we would worry about the payment of the cards once we were back and have sold our house.

Our decision to move to America was by now not a secret anymore and I could freely share my dreams with friends, family and colleagues. The reaction from most of them was very much the same: "You are so lucky", they said.

Some of them admired our faith and prayed us God-speed while others were intrigued by the thought of me leaving my senior manager position for a very uncertain future. They found it astonishing that my position in the bank was not nearly as important to me as the future of my children.

My greatest concern was the effect our decision was going to have on my mother, who was 76 years old. Somehow we knew that Karen's mom would handle it well, especially that she was an experienced traveler and would visit us whenever she could.

My mother was not all that shocked when I told her very hesitantly. I suppose the social climate in the country contributed a great deal to her understanding. She wanted to know whether we thought it well through and when I told her that we not only thought it well through, but also prayed about it, she was satisfied. I emphasized my decision by reminding her that my dad always cared a great deal for his children and under the circumstances may have done the same.

We managed to get a flight on the 21st of September, flying Alitalia from Johannesburg to Rome and from there to New York, where we were instructed to hand our documents to the American immigration authorities.

I called Norman to get ideas about our period of stay and accommodation and as always, they were ready with encouragement and guidance.

Blessing Number 11.   Dude and Novie

The answer was simple, yet very practical.

Dude and Novie Burton took care of Dude's mother's house after she passed away, and the house was standing empty at the time. They offered us the house to live in for free, as long as we could find basic furniture. That was easy, because we knew that we were going to need furniture in the States anyway and we could therefore buy the absolute necessary items during our visit. The house had a stove and refrigerator and all we really had to add was beds and bedding. Dude and Novie brought an old lounge suite and Norman provided an old TV.

The trip was a new experience for Melissa, as she was the only one of the family who had never been out of South Africa before.

We flew from Johannesburg to Rome, from Rome to Newark, from Newark to Charlotte in North Carolina and from there to Chattanooga, Tennessee. We had 14 suitcases with us. We were trying to bring as many of our valuable personal belongings with us as we could and planned to leave some of it with Norman and Joyce until we made our final trip.

We had all our papers ready for the immigration authorities at Newark airport, but we were all still very skeptical and nervous.

Thinking about it now, our faith was still not strong enough to handle those insecurities, yet we strongly believed that it was God's plan for us to move to America.

Karen was the only one who needed to have her photo's redone because she was wearing little earrings when they took it in South Africa, and the Americans did not like that. So they took new photographs of her at the airport and within thirty minutes we were out of there.

They stamped our passports, giving us temporary residence. Our green cards would be mailed to us. We were relieved as we realized that we were halfway there and the excitement was clear as we were boarding our next flight. Melissa sat next to a gentleman called Mike on the flight from Newark to Charlotte and the two were chatting away like old friends. He gave her some M&M's and that really made her day.

Norman and Joyce were waiting for us in Chattanooga, and once we got the rented car we had booked, we were on our way to Sand Mountain, Alabama.

By now we were experts in handling the load of luggage we were transporting, and having two cars available, made it easier. We were very tired from the lengthy flights and naturally all the stress of all the uncertainties, but we started feeling relief in realizing that it was only a matter of time before our ultimate goal was reached.

We stayed with Norman and Joyce for a few days, played cards and did our shopping. On Monday, 25th September 1994, Karen, Norman and I went to Gadsden, Alabama where we applied for our social security cards. Once again we were playing the waiting game: waiting for our green cards and social security cards to arrive.

Blessing Number 12.   Buying a car

It was time for us to get our own transportation, as the rented car was too expensive to keep for a lengthy period of time. Norman and I have been visiting used auto dealers and I have made up my mind to buy a car in Boaz, Alabama.

On our way back from Gadsden, I decided that it was a convenient time to get the car, so we took the 431 from Gadsden to Boaz. As we were entering Boaz, I noticed a canary yellow car on a stand at a used dealer shop. I decided to have a closer look, but it turn out to be one of those who were nice from far but far from nice.

I discovered that it was another of the Lord's ploys to attract my attention as I found a beautifully, well-cared-for 1985 Buick Somerset for a very reasonable price. I had my travel checks with me and within 20 minutes drove away in our very first American car. The car was a much better deal than any other car we considered before and we were again convinced that the Lord wanted us to have it and we praised His holy Name for it.

Blessing Number 13.   Selling our house

We assigned a real estate agent in South Africa to try and sell our house for us while we were gone, as time was limited.

Our house in Constantia Kloof, Johannesburg

We knew that the timing in selling was much more critical than the price we got for it. Agent's commission in S.A. is high and we needed any penny we could get, but we realized that actually finding a buyer was priority number one and somehow the final figure did not matter that much. The agent had about four months to try and find a buyer and conclude the total deal. While it may sound a fair period of time, we knew that in the real estate market it was not really all that long.

I found a shop in Fort Payne from where I could send and receive faxes and that sorted out my communication with the agent.

We were hardly a week away from home when we received a message that there was a fax for us. It turned out to be an offer on our house.

We were delighted! Although the offer was not quite as much as we were hoping for, it was a solid offer with a guaranteed mortgage loan for the buyer. It did not take us long to make up our minds and we faxed back, accepting the offer.

One more possible stumbling block was out of the way and another point was added to our list of blessings.

The period we stayed in America turned out to be fun-filled as the pressure of selling the house was gone and we could concentrate on less stressful issues. We found a furniture shop with reasonable prices and bought two double beds and one twin size.

The girls had to share the one double bed as we planned to purchase another bed later. Buying the bedding and a few kitchen utensils was fun as we had enough money to pick and chose. We decided to do without anything that was not absolutely necessary and rather buy better quality items of things we needed.

The house we lived in was fine and well situated. We did however have some fun in chasing and catching tiny mice that must have looked at us as intruders in a place they have occupied for an unknown period of time. These adventures helped to lift our spirits as the thought of moving from our family, friends and country did dampen the spirits at times.

The church members at Ider were friendly and helpful and that also comforted us.

We received our social security cards within about two weeks and this sealed our move to the States. Up to this point everything focused on applications, but the social security cards gave us the permission to work in America, which put us a notch above the normal visitors to the country.

It was time for us to get back to South Africa as we still had a great deal of business to attend to.

We were told that it was going to take about six to eight weeks before we could expect our green cards. The stamps in our passports were enough for us to go in and out of the country and therefore we did not mind waiting.

Again Norman and Joyce were there to transport us to the airport in Chattanooga and this time Dude and Novie came with to see us off. We felt spoilt and stood amazed at the way God was using others to help us along.

The first house in Henagar, Alabama that Dude and Novie Burton gave us to live in for our temporary stay in 1994.

CHAPTER 7.

THE LAST TWO MONTHS

We left most of our luggage with Norman and Joyce and took as many of the empty cases we could with us back to South Africa. We still had a lot of personal belongings that we wanted to bring to the States, and we needed every possible suitcase as we could handle. Smaller cases were put inside the bigger ones to make things easier. One of my work colleagues met us with my company car at the airport and soon we were home and the next phase started.

The previous 3 months flew by and we still had a number of decisions to make. We had to consider whether it was worth our while to ship our furniture to the States. Although the furniture was in pretty good shape, we had to weigh up the cost of shipping plus what we could sell it for, against the cost of buying new furniture. I made a list of approximate values on my computer to see if I could come up with an answer. We realized that we would have to sell all of the electrical appliances, as the electric current used in the States is 110 voltage compared to the 220 voltage in South Africa.

Blessing Number 14.   Selling our furniture

It was Monday afternoon and I was at work when Karen called me. Linda Snyman, a school teacher and a dear friend of ours, was visiting with Karen at home and wanted to know if we did not want to sell a set of oak chairs we had. I told Karen that once we started selling furniture, we needed to sell everything. It was not worth our while to ship only a few items overseas. We decided to see how successful we would be in selling our furniture and how much we could get for it. Without my knowledge, Wayne told Karen about my inventory list on the computer and by the Thursday, most of the bigger items had would-be buyers. I could not contest the prices, as they thought my inventory list was what I wanted, instead of a minimum value that I noted for my own benefit.

Melissa and Linda's daughter Lauren wanted to have a yard sale and I helped them to put a table and some items for sale out on our drive-run. There was a taxi stop across the road from our house and many of the gardeners and other people working in the neighborhood, took note of the yard sale. We told them that it was not the real thing as we were planning a major sale the following Saturday at 9 am.

Melissa and Lauren sold most of the items on their list and that seemed to inspire Melissa for greater things. On Friday, the day before the planned yard sale, I arrived home from work at about 5.45pm. I was hardly home when the doorbell rang. It was some of the local black people who came to see if we were not prepared to sell some of the items planned for the next day. They were scared that everything would be sold out before they could get there the next day.

The next 2 hours turned out to be chaotic, to say the least. We had more people in our house than we have had for a long time and everyone was standing ready with cash in their hands to purchase anything they could. We adjusted prices as we were going along to offer good deals to those that bought more than one item. There were even those who paid ahead of time for furniture that we still needed until we leave.

After most of them had finally left, I walked into the kitchen and Natalie was standing at the sink. "Dad," she said: " the Lord is moving to fast for me now." It sounded so good and I was so uplifted by my daughter's recognition of God's hand in our fortune that I could feel my emotions building up. So I hugged her and thanked God in my heart for our blessings.

The planned yard sale for the Saturday was cancelled for we had no more items to sell. One gentleman even bought all the tools and junk I was hoarding over the years in my garage. That saved me the trouble of having to dump it somewhere after we had vacated the house. Saturday morning at 7:30am the bell rang again and there were more people inquiring about articles to buy. I told them that everything was sold, but one lady literally searched all our kitchen cupboards and inquired about each utensil she found in there. So we sold basically everything we collected over 21 years, within one week.

Christopher, the gardener who worked for us on a bi-weekly basis, received quite a number of items for free but, I decided to sell him one of my new mohair suits for R25 (about $7) and he promised to pay me the next week. We were keeping Wayne's new mountain bike as a Christmas gift for Christopher, but great was our disappointment when

Christopher never came back to pay for the suit. We eventually sold the bike for R400 (about $120).

One of the more expensive items we needed to sell was Karen's 1985 Volkswagen Golf. Great was our surprise when we had three potential buyers within two weeks. My brother-in-law eventually bought it for my nephew and paid us in advance.

At no point in time during all this trading, did we experience any difficulty in either selling any item or collecting the money for it. The Lord knew that we needed the funds and that there was no time for difficulties.

Blessing Number 15.   A home for our pets

We also had two young dogs and we knew that they could not come with us, so after careful inquiries, one of my young employees, who was still living with his parents, offered to take both of them. That seemed to put the family's minds at ease for we knew that they had a good home. We still felt sad about having to get rid of our pets although we understood that this move was going to cost us more than just money.

Blessing Number 16.   Norman's phone call

We received a call from Norman telling us that our green cards have finally arrived at Ider. We had to give their mailing address, for we were not sure how long it would take and where we would be at the time the cards arrive. We also did not want to take any chances with the mail service between America and South Africa. These green cards were far too precious to us to take the chance of it getting lost in the mail. The cards meant that we finally got our permanent residence in the United States and the answer to many prayers.

Blessing Number 17.   Our own spiritual growth

I asked the family to prepare themselves for a devotion, where we as a family could praise the Lord and thank Him collectively for what He has done for us. Each person brought a scripture to the table and conveyed his or her understanding of the scripture to the family.

First it was Karen. She reminded us of Matthew 6 and the lilies of the field. God will always take care of us as long as we recognize Him in whatever we plan and we will not have to worry about tomorrow.

Natalie chose Psalm 23. The Lord is my Shepherd and while He is there we have nothing to fear.

Wayne found a passage in Luke 14 reminding us that to be a disciple of Christ means to be prepared to give up the material things of this life, if that is what is required.

Melissa read part of the Lord's Prayer in Matthew 6. "Give us this day our daily bread and forgive us our trespasses..".

I concluded by reading verses from Psalm 40 for them: "I waited patiently for the Lord; He turned to me and heard my cry. He lifted me out of the slimy pit, out of the mud and mire; He set my feet on a rock and gave me a firm place to stand. He put a new song in my mouth, a hymn of praise to our God."

Yes, God did that for me and He did it for us as a family. So we bowed our heads and thanked Him.

I told one of the ladies at church about our experiences and how the Lord has opened doors for us. "It's amazing!" she said, "It's sounds too good to be true".

"No" I replied, "When God is involved, you bet it is possible and true!" We came to realize that faith can surely bring forth what otherwise may seem impossible. We were busy moving mountains just as Jesus had promised us.

Blessing Number 18. Assistance from the human resources department

I started doing my last financial planning before we finally had to leave South Africa. I had to make arrangements for the money in my pension fund to be invested in an annuity in South Africa, as we were not permitted to draw on it for 10 years. I was surprised at the friendly co-operation I got from the human resources department of First National Bank, the company I worked for. These people had every reason to perform their other duties first and yet, in every request I put to them, they assisted me as if I was the most valuable employee they had.

The last memorable event in our house was the farewell party Melissa had for her school friends. We gave her permission to invite 17 girls from her class at school and they all planned to sleep over the night.

The biggest mistake I ever made in my life! They had to sleep wherever they could find a convenient spot and for some of them it was obviously not very comfortable. Some were crying because of Melissa leaving, some were crying because they were uncomfortable, others were crying because some were nasty and others still had time for mischief. I was doing pajama drill and it was early hours of the morning when I finally threatened to call some parents, as my patience were just about gone.

That seemed to have the required effect and the event ended peacefully, but I vowed never to get myself in a spot like that again.

CHAPTER 8.

ACCOMMODATION FOR ONE MONTH

B lessing Number 19. Living in someone else's house

Our house was sold and we had until the end of November 1994 to live there. One of the potential problems was our accommodation in South Africa immediately prior to our departure, but we were aware of that and considered various options. We finally decided on the one opportunity that was not only the most inexpensive, but also the most valuable during that critical period of time.

Dear friends of ours, Dawie and Annatjie Venter, invited us to live with them in their house until it was time for us to leave. They had a bigger than average size house and one of their two daughters was already married and not living with them anymore.

Dawie and I were not only great spiritual brothers but have also spent many hours on the golf course together. We grabbed this opportunity, as it was going to give as extra time with our friends of some 17 years. We only had the luggage we were planning to take overseas with us and although it was another 14 suitcases, it was easy enough to store for one month. Moving out of our house was not much of an issue as we were never really too attached to any physical environment.

Dawie and his family had a vacation planned during that time. It was therefore convenient for them having us in their home and being able to take care of it while they were away. When they finally came back around Christmas, we enjoyed our time together in doing everything good friends do - fruitful discussions of life and life here after, watching sport and other programs on TV, playing golf and eating out. We enjoyed watermelon and barbecue together and all of us joint in the preparations and cooking wherever possible. We just had a great time and we got to know each other just a little bit better and felt sorry that we did not do more of those things together in the years before when we had so much more time.

We lived with Dawie & Annatjie Venter for one month.

Blessing Number 20.   Jan helps us.

Jan Korsten, another dear friend and fellow Christian, visited with us one evening in Dawie's house. Jan was a chartered accountant and I took the opportunity in discussing the requirements of the revenue department with him knowing that Jan could possibly give me some advice. We looked at the tax clearance forms and Jan pointed out to me that we required a South African sponsor to take care of any possible outstanding tax issues after we have left the country. Not having too many people to consider in such a short period of time, I asked Jan if he could possibly do it for us and he agreed without hesitation. This was a great relieve to us as any delay with the tax clearance would delay our access to the funds we were hoping to take out of the country. The old saying of "a friend in need is a friend indeed" had some meaning for us again.

The month of December is summer time in South Africa and also an ideal time for shopping. We made a list of nice-to-haves and also necessary items which we wanted to take to the States with us. The only thing that limited us in buying a lot more was not money this time, but the knowledge that we were limited in packing space and restricted in weight on the plane. We bought things like custard and curry powder and "Five Roses" teabags. We knew that we were allowed to bring that into the States and knowing that those particular items were hard to come by outside of South Africa, we purchased enough to last us as long as possible. We also bought some natural remedies that we have come to trust and relied on, and we wanted to make sure that we had some available, should we ever need it. Included in this was, "Rooi Laventel", a stomach cramp remedy and "Albus" for a blocked nose.

Blessing Number 21.   Tax clearance

We had to wait for my final paycheck before we could apply for tax clearance. We did not want to have any unrecorded income to complicate the clearance of the funds we needed to take with us. Once Jan signed the documents as sponsor, Karen was ready to take it to the revenue department for processing. We were told that this process may take up to three weeks and knowing how some of the government departments operate, we were expecting a six weeks waiting period before we would have our tax clearance certificates. Luckily, we were able to take a fair sum of money out of the country as normal travel allowance, and that would have bought us some time.

Again, there was a surprise waiting for us. Karen presented the application forms and explained to the lady the details of our plans. Well, this lady was not going to be any less significant in God's plan and within 30 minutes Karen left the revenue department with the tax clearance certificates in her hand! When God does something, He does it well.

Blessing Number 22.   The final flight arrangements

We booked our final flight well ahead of time to ensure that we could leave South Africa as early as possible in 1995. The children needed to start school in America without any unnecessary delay. The cost and timing of the flight was important to us and eventually we managed to secure seats on a British Airways flight, due to leave South Africa on January 10, 1995. We were hoping to leave a few days earlier, and also on a cheaper flight, but all those were fully booked. The travel agent did however put us on stand-by on a Sabena flight that was scheduled to leave January 5. This flight was not only on an earlier date, but would also save us about R2000 ($600).

About two weeks before this flight, the lady at the travel agency called me to say that there have been cancellations and we had tickets for the earlier and cheaper flight. By now, we were not at all surprised at this good fortune and treated it as something we expected. The Lord has proved it so many times, that it became the rule instead of the exception.

Blessing Number 23.   Our money comes through

Everything was happening as we were hoping and it was evident that there was a great Hand steering this ship. One of the main issues was still outstanding though - the deal in the sale of our house was still being finalized and we were waiting in anticipation for the closing procedures. We had one week before we were due to leave and the money from our house was badly needed for us to resettle and also to assist in living expenses. Again the anxiety was uncalled for, as the lawyers did the final closing and the payout on Friday, December 29, 1994 and we were ready for the United States of America. After paying all the outstanding bills, we were left with about R128, 000 ($41,000 at the time) to take with us. We had to leave more behind in annuities, but will hopefully get the benefit of that some day.

I made the effort in adding up the cost of all the trips and expenses we incurred during the last two years in preparation for this move. The total amount was about R58, 000 (about $18,000) and that did not include the loss in having to sell our house, furniture and endowment policies prematurely. On top of this all, I gave up senior management position, a career that took me roughly 20 years of hard work to achieve. So I had to ask myself whether it was worth it all and although I did not have the final answer at the time, never let it worry me.

Blessing Number 24.   Saying good-bye

Time for saying goodbye was coming closer and closer and we were dreading it. Most of the family members were living near Cape Town, while we were in Johannesburg, - a 1,000 miles away. So we found ourselves in a situation where we knew that we would not be able to see everyone before we leave. We were still busy with our final arrangements and I still had to work until December 31.

Karen's car was sold and I had to hand my company car back. We were therefore without reliable transportation and would have had to rent a car or borrow one from someone, if we wanted to make a trip to Cape Town. Renting was expensive and we thought it better for one of the children and I to fly and visit my mom before we leave. We knew that Karen's mom could come and visit us and since it was not that long ago since we have seen her last, the need to see my mom got priority.

When I phoned my mom to tell her about our idea, she was not at all excited. I discovered later that she could not face the thought of saying goodbye and being sickly and old, decided that we would honor her wishes and said our good-byes over the phone. Having lived that far away from them all the years, and only being able to see them but once a year, helped to make the situation a bit easier, although we would still have preferred to spent time with each of them. Knowing that my mother could always do with some more money due to continuous medical bills, we decided to send her the money we would have had to pay for the air tickets.

At church it turned out to be worse. We were due to leave on Thursday, January 5, 1995. Wednesday evening was our normal midweek Bible study. We decided to make it a singing evening and as song leader, I was invited to lead the occasion. I wanted to let the members at Weltevreden Park Church of Christ know how much I loved them all and how we are going to miss them, and that we will always remember them wherever we are.

So on the spur of the moment; I decided to lead each individual's favorite song. I did not have to ask them to nominate it, as I could do it from memory. They appreciated it and at the end of the service showed it in tears. I often wonder how God looked upon farewells like that and if there was maybe just a little sadness in heaven as well, while friends were hugging each other down here below.

CHAPTER 9.

WE ARE LEAVING SOUTH AFRICA

The day finally arrived for us to leave our country and move to a new home, far, far away. We had to use Dawie's small truck to transport the luggage to the airport. Bob Pearce played taxi for the family and great was our delight when a number of our friends took off from work to see us off. All the tears were shed the night before and by now we were all in a fairly happy mood, although the hugs were long and warm when our flight departure was announced.

Arriving in Brussels, our first stop, it was white with snow and as snow was hardly ever seen in South Africa, we were excited, especially being able to walk on it. This excitement did not last long as we learned that our next flight to London was delayed by 90 minutes because of ice on the airplane. What made it worse was that nobody cared about us moving to the States, as nobody seemed to be in a hurry.

Thinking about it, it was not a chartered flight and we were the only ones on the plane aware of this major event in our lives!

London brought us a great amount of anxiety. We landed at Heathrow Airport and had to take a bus from there to Gatwick from where our flight for New York was leaving. The delay in Brussels caused us pressed for time to get to Gatwick on time. My blood pressure must have been sky-high and the tiredness from the previous 14 hours flying and not sleeping all that much, did not make it any better. We literally ran with our wagonload of luggage when the bus arrived at Gatwick and great was our relief when the personnel from Continental Airlines were ready for us and, twenty minutes before take-off, we were all on board.

We could finally relax when the plane eventually took off for America. Everyone was tired and tried to rest as best possible. Nothing really exciting happened on the flight and landing was just like any other arrival of a flight. We were not sure whether we were going to face any difficulties from the airport authorities, as we were reliant on the stamps in our passports to give us entry into the country and considering that our green cards were with the Flynns in Alabama. The young man at the terminal counter was friendly and let us through without any problems.

The people at customs were a bit nosy at the loads of luggage we had with us, but we had nothing to declare or hide, so no problems there either. It was while handling this luggage at Newark airport, that I hurt a tendon in my shoulder and suffered with it for a year to come. I figured later that it was the hurry we were in and the tiredness, which caused me to hurt myself.

From Newark, we departed for Atlanta. The weather was bad and we had quite a bumpy flight. When we arrived in Atlanta, I went to Hertz to get a rented van, for we knew that a car would be too small. Karen and the kids were looking out for our luggage.

We waited and waited and 30 minutes later we discovered that our luggage was delayed and would arrive on the next flight. We decided that our day was by now long enough, we were tired and needed proper sleep, so we told the airline personnel to deliver our luggage to us the next day - so we got in the van and headed for Ider, Alabama.

The roads were wet and at times I could hardly keep my eyes open. We drove carefully and stopped occasionally, and safely got to Ider at 10:30pm that evening, 36 hours after we left Johannesburg. (There is an 8-hour time difference during winter between Johannesburg and Ider).

Norman and Joyce were relieved to see us safely arriving and like always, the tea was hot and waiting, just like we South Africans like it. The reunion of our friendship and the comfortable beds, were even better.

The Gerbers have arrived and the United States was never going to be the same again.

CHAPTER 10.

THE FIRST SIX MONTHS
IN A FOREIGN LAND

We had a long list of errands to run, once in America. Norman and Joyce again shared their home with us and we knew that finding a permanent place to live has to be priority number one. We were a big family and we did not want to intrude on them unnecessary. Norman wanted us to stay some time with them and we all agreed that we would stay a maximum of one week, if the Lord permits.

We took the kids to school on Monday where we met the principal, Mr. Gann and the counselor, Ms. Haynes. The children each got assigned a buddy and their school career in America officially kicked off. They each gained about 6 months due to the difference in school calendars between South Africa and the United States. We later learned that the first month was the most horrible time our children ever experienced in their lives. They were trying not to miss their old friends too much, make new friends and above all, get used to a school system that was drastically different from the highly disciplined system they were accustomed to. They did however enjoy getting bonus points for extra efforts and often breaking the 100% mark in school tests, was a new, pleasant experience!

Settling in the United States of America was an exciting business, but at no point was it so exciting that we forgot who made it possible for us. We remembered all of the many blessings we received in South Africa and as we were working towards a permanent abode in the States, it became time again to count those special big blessings.

Blessing Number 25.   We find a house to rent

We had one week to find a house to rent on Sand Mountain and the choices were limited. This was not a city where facilities like that may be specially catered for, but a rural community where houses are either lived in or sold. Norman told us of a gentleman by the name of Jerry Stubbs, the local pharmacist, who may have some houses for rent. Jerry had two houses available, but someone else had already booked the one, so we were left with only one to choice. The house was tiny and out in the woods and the thought of living out there made me miserable. I was hoping that we would be able to live under reasonable conditions and this house and environment did not represent "reasonable" to me.

Our first rented house in Henagar, Alabama.

Having thought about our choices, Karen and I decided that we will take it until something better becomes available. The next day I went to pay the deposit to secure it and I told Jerry straight out that I did not like the idea of living out there, but as I had no choice, will take it. Great was my relief when he told me that the other people did not pay their deposit and for that reason I could have the other, if I so wish. We quickly took a ride out to where this house was and although the house was rather small and simple looking, we were quite excited to get it, because this one was at least situated on the main road.

Blessing Number 26.   Assistance to settle

We started shopping for furniture and found one or two places with good quality furniture, at reasonable prices. We bought most of it from Thomas & Son in Powell and they did an excellent job in delivering everything promptly. We bought our washing machine, tumble dryer and freezer from Coopers in Valley Head and again the service was excellent. Our beds were still at the house that Dude and Novie Burton housed us in and Tommy Laney was ready to use his truck to move it for us. We found this kind of friendliness and assistance comforting, while we were trying to find our feet.

Again God was using each and everybody to help us in our daily needs.

Everyone that we came in contact with immediately recognized that we were not from Alabama and our accents must have been sounding strange to all. I have the tendency to speak fast and that made it even more difficult for the Southeners to understand. I must admit that their way of using the English language was also very colorful to us and at times we could not help but to smile. Our children, especially Wayne, quickly picked up this Southern accent and way of speaking and when he started talking about "them shoes" or "I am fixing to do this or that" we could not resist teasing him.

I did not grow up speaking English and was taught it at school and therefore tend to be very aware of using the correct grammar (although nowadays I have picked up some bad habits myself). I found the general use of grammar quite shocking while in comparison the vocabulary of the Alabamians, was beautiful. My favorite phrase I learned from them is: "I am very proud for you". We have always been "proud of" someone but never "for". We became familiar with terms such as "hillbilly" and "redneck".

Blessing Number 27.   Karen finds a job

Karen and I started participating in all possible church activities following our arrival in Ider. On Thursdays some of us would go and visit some old folks at a nearby nursing home and we found great blessings and spiritual encouragement in doing that. It was terrible to see the state in which some old people find themselves and no kinfolk to visit and comfort them. We were far away from all the old people in South Africa that we loved, and so we shared some of our valuable time with these foreign people. We would sing for them and those that could still read or remembered the songs would join in. They found it hard to let us go once the visitation hour was over and we could not help to feel sad for them. We often wonder what kind of person could leave his or her mother or father with total strangers and never visited them and we thanked God for the love He taught us and the compassion we still possessed.

We were missing our family and friends in South Africa and Karen was very loyal in writing to many of them as often as she had time. I wrote occasional letters to my mom and three sisters and also phoned them from time to time, although it was a bit expensive.

I decided that had I to let the congregation at Weltevreden Park know that I still cared for them, so I wrote them a poem and mailed it to Bob and Angie Pearce with one of Karen's letters. It was not very professional, but it said what was in my heart and I hope they have kept it, but if they did not have, I still have:

TO MY FRIENDS AND BRETHREN
AT WELTEVREDEN PARK

I think of you, friends
Far over the seas,
While I am working
Or down on my knees.

I love you and miss you
And want you to know,
My thoughts are with you
Wherever you go.

At least I know
That the Lord does care
For all of us
And for all of you there.

So keep the faith
And trust in the Lord
And do not forget
To study His Word.

For He will never
Let you down
And will one day reward you
With His royal crown.

Love,
Chris Gerber

Karen applied for a job at a local factory that made children's clothing and got the job. She had never worked in a factory before, but we thought it time to find additional income. All the expenses were adding up and we wanted to keep as much as possible of our own money as a deposit for a house.

The activities at the church were not taking much of our time and I found myself looking for something challenging - similar to what I was so used to during all my years in applications development. We also needed more income and I started looking for a full-time job.

Blessing Number 28.   Helping Computer Solutions

While in Fort Payne one day, I saw the building of Computer Solutions and decided that I could possibly make a contribution in a company like that. Tim Clothier, the owner, was a friendly man and when I told him that I could possibly assist him with managerial practices and especially business plans, he invited me to help him on a consultancy basis. I liked the idea as it was still giving me the freedom to participate in various church activities. This part time position helped me to learn the American way of doing things, while also adding a small income. I learned about computer hardware, while I helped Tim to understand some of the more up-to-date management principles, something I had a fair amount of training and experience in.

Living in that small house was fine - most of the time. I said "most of the time", as we quickly discovered that it was a little too far from the Ider High School and outside of the school bus routes. We were therefore personally responsible to get the kids to school and back and as we only had one car, the transport became a bit of a problem.

We decided that we had no choice but to purchase another car and so went ahead and bought a 1988 Buick Lesabre.

We experienced our first snow in the United States of America, but luckily for us, the winter was reasonably mild and nothing really to write home about.

Blessing Number 29.   Getting our own house

We had signed a lease contract for six months for the house and decided that it would be a good time to move closer to the school, if possible, when the lease expires. We had more time now and started looking out for advertising boards or notices for rental property.

Wayne started playing football. It was a new experience for him and very different from the rugby he played in South Africa, but he enjoyed it and was quickly dedicated to the expectations of the coach.

It was one afternoon in April, while fetching him from school after practice, when we noticed a house that was up for sale. This house was within walking distance from the school. We had often noticed a gentleman in the mornings having a cup of coffee on the front porch of this house, while driving to school. I told Wayne that while I know that it was too early for us to be successful in obtaining a mortgage bond, I wanted to see what the house was like and how much the owner were hoping to get for it.

The house had three bedrooms and a den and one and a half bathroom and was situated on two acres of land. It had a carport for two cars, as well as a very big double garage that the owner built for storing his boat.

We were impressed, but thought it possibly out of our reach. Billy Gann was a friendly man and I told him about us having moved from South Africa and looking for a better place to stay, preferably a house we could buy. He wanted $70,000 for the house and I told him that I had the 20% deposit, but he would have to carry the financing himself, because no bank would lend us any money just yet. Again I was not much surprised when Billy told me that he would consider it, but that he needed to speak to Bobby, his wife.

I somehow knew the deal was done and hurried home to tell Karen that I found us a house. We went back to the house so she could see for herself and although this house was not the greatest and smartest, we knew that this was what the Lord had kept for us and the financial contract turned out to be just a formality. Bobby told us later that she had tears as she agreed to sell the house she lived in for many years, but she thanked the Lord that she could play a part in finding a home for us.

We are still thankful for God-fearing people like Billy and Bobby Gann who put enough trust in us to finance the house for us and we pray God's blessings on them.

We signed the contract on 22nd April 1995, but we could only move in on June 1. This time the move was much bigger as we had accumulated nearly a house full of furniture and there was still those many suitcases of luggage, some of which we had not unpacked yet.

Again the brethren at the Church stood ready to help us and with Tommy and Carol Laney, Ron and Chris Anderson assisting us, we soon had everything moved and put into place.

We felt like real Americans now, owning our own house in the United States. We converted the den into a bedroom so that each of the children may have his own bedroom and life seemed to become a bit easier.

Finally our own house in Ider, Alabama.

Blessing Number 30.   God-given neighbors

The Southerners must be some of the most godly and generous people that the good Lord has created. People, who we have never met us before, turned up at our door with vegetables and words of kindness to welcome us in the neighborhood. Our immediate neighbors were Opella Smith and Marvin and Lois Moody, and to find more kind and friendlier people, a person will have to search a long while.

Everything about the purchase of this house seemed so perfect and well planned that it would take a fool to deny the hand of Deity in it. We again realized that God does not hide Himself, but it is only us who close our eyes that made it impossible sometimes for us to see Him. We learned never to search for signs like the Jews did according to 1Corinthians 1, but to look rather for the effect of a living God in the practical things of life and somehow we got to see a lot more of Him.

Blessing Number 31.   Helping Rainbow congregation

Things in the Church did not go as well for us as we were hoping. We soon discovered that the freedom that we enjoyed at Weltevreden Park in exploring scriptures during Bible study, was very limited. I put my foot in it when I suggested during one study, that we need to open our minds more and look for all possible meaning of scripture, rather than be dogmatic about something only because we grew up with it. I learned that philosophy 22 years ago when I discovered that not everything that my parents taught us was scriptural and while they were the best parents anybody ever had, they were also fallible and traditions could easily cloud one's mind and understanding.

"Search the scriptures daily like the Bereans did in Acts 17 and we may all be found well-pleasing unto God" was my plea, but when I used an example of different opinions one may have of a given subject, I was a marked man who apparently taught unscriptural things. The sad part was that no-one ever bothered to discuss the issue further with me to try and understand what I was saying and that I ever taught anyone "unscriptural" things were as far from the truth as anything. So when I got invited to assist a nearby congregation with song leading and preaching, I jumped at the opportunity.

The congregation at Rainbow, Sylvania only had about 30 members, but we found it an ideal place to worship God and I got to do everything in the church I ever wanted and the spiritual fellowship we enjoyed, turned out to be the best remedy for the difficult year ahead.

CHAPTER 11.

GOD TEACHES US HUMILITY

Blessing Number 32.   Learning experiences in a sock mill

The next eleven months were the biggest learning experience of our lives. I was still looking for full-time employment and a friend of ours at Ider, Vince Laney, offered me a job at a sock mill where he was one of the managers. The idea was that I would learn the sock business so that I progress to a supervisor or manager position. I was quite willing as it was not only additional income, but Fort Payne was the sock capital of the world and we were only living 20 miles away from it. I believed that if anyone was going to live in the area, he or she should at least know a little bit of the industry.

At this time I was already busy with a correspondence training course at the National State Training College which helped me to understand American government and other general subjects. So I was eager to learn the "socking" business. There was just one big snag - I would have to work third shift as a boarder. The impact of that decision only hit me later and with a bang, but I have never been some-one who was status conscious or scared of sweating a bit, so third shift boarding was what was going to get me to understand the sock industry.

137

When I turned up at 10.45 p.m. on June 12, 1995 for my first night shift, I was mentally prepared for it but what I found nearly sent me home. The supervisor, Don Crocker, had to get the shift started before he could give me any attention. There I was standing in the middle of the night for two hours, a man with 10 years management, of which 7 years as senior manager, experience behind him and well trained, waiting to do a blue collar job, while his family has gone to bed.
I remembered what I promised God many years ago: "I will do anything if you let us go" and I remembered the story of Jephthah and his daughter in the book of Judges.

When I finally got some attention, a young lady was appointed to teach me the art of boarding - taking socks out of a big buggy and fit it over something like a big flat hot metal foot to shape the sock. The socks were on a rotating wheel and the machine would automatically peel the sock off, where it would be paired and packaged. We were being paid by the dozen pairs, about 19 cents on average per dozen pairs.

Just imagine, placing 24 socks on a rotary board, which was hot enough to burn you if you touch it, and be paid 19 cents for it. I could not help but to think about my secretary, company car with free gasoline, company credit card, and all the senior manager privileges which I took so for granted in South Africa and I learned my first lesson in the sock mill - let us receive what God give us with thanksgiving, whatever it is.

The young lady was friendly and patient and sometimes a little too much at ease as the odors indicated, but we got along just fine and by the second evening, I was ready to do the job by myself. A number of the younger people wanted to know what I was doing there and I realized that there was something about me that appeared out of place, and it was not my age. Some were looking to see how long I was going to last in this very close to miserable environment, but it was now that the hardships I endured as a child started paying dividends and it was not long before I started producing the same kind of totals as what they were used to - over 400 dozen in an 8-hour shift. I often had to take IB-Profen tablets for sore muscles, but other than my shoulder that was still hurting from the injured tendon, I survived the physical agony.

The physical agony was nothing compared to the mental agony. I had 8 hours, every night, to stand and think - and think, and think. I started looking for opportunities to use my experience and make a contribution that way to the company, but nobody expected that from a boarder and while all my proposals were accepted in a friendly manner, the lack of implementation of some of my ideas taught me that it was not as important to them as to me and I was wasting my time. So I stopped thinking for the company.

I often had the opportunity to share our experiences with some-body like Don, as he would often come and just stand and talk to me while I was working. I found a great need to express my gratitude to our Lord for what He had done for us and Don said to me one night: "Chris, the Lord will always take care of you because you are so prepared to give Him all the glory". I felt so happy and the encouragement meant so much to me. My family and my friends were 9000 miles away, but I knew that God was real close and I thanked Him for it.

Many nights I would stand there and prepare Bible lessons in my head. I have always liked to apply scriptural meaning to real life issues, very much like Jesus did in the teaching of the parables. While considering certain management principles, I came upon the idea of applying modern day management principles to the leadership style that Jesus applied.

I was amazed. He appointed his own team. He lead with authority, yet was always with them as part of the team. He made sure they had the training and tools. He gave them clear goals and applied situational leadership, being gentle at times and tough at other times. He organized to perfection and motivated constantly. He warned them of the risks and took precautions against it. He even planned for the time when He was gone. And I thought: "What a manager! What a God! I could not find a better one in my life!"

Karen joint me a month later at the sock mill. We heard that Buster Brown, the company she worked for, was closing down and moving operations to Mexico, so she got herself a job as a turn sewer at the sock mill. She adapted pretty well to the environment but the daytime sleeping gave both of us lots of problems. We found it difficult to rest properly, having to sleep from 8 am to whatever time in the afternoon. Although our house is about 50 yards from the road, we found the traffic noise disturbing.

One morning we were woken up by an ear-piercing noise. Our neighbor was busy vacuuming his yard. I tried my best to be as nice as I could when I went to ask him if it would matter if he did that job a little later in the day. He was kind as always and apologized, but I felt bad.

We developed a daily routine that still sometimes haunt us. Every evening before we would leave for work, we would watch the

Nickelodeon channel and especially "Welcome back, Kotter" (I loved Vini Babarino), and most mornings we would stop at Jack's in Fort Payne for breakfast, pancakes and syrup. We watched "Bewitched" and then went to sleep.

The children were big enough to look after themselves but we still did not care much for the idea of leaving them at night by themselves. It was during the winter of 1995/1996 that our children experienced the night of their lives. Sand Mountain experienced a terrible icy winter and many trees fell, one very close to our house. The kids were woken 2 am by the cracking noises of branches breaking and trees falling. They investigated and comforted one another and we thanked God for keeping them safe.

The trees fell on power lines and telephone wires and we were stranded for 5 days without electricity. We had to cook our food and boil water on a gas barbecue grill. We were not at all prepared for such and event and had to borrow a gas heater from friends of ours. We closed off part of the house and all of us slept in the living room to be close to the heater. The kids went to sleep with Lynn and Eric Woods for a night or two and that alleviated the hardship of the experience some for them.

Karen and I still tried to get to work even though the roads were iced up and treacherous in places. Our fellow-workers were amazed at our dedication and we were proud to show them that we were not scared of work and hardships. One morning on our way back home, we go stuck halfway up a hill and could not move forward or backward because to the ice on the road. We eventually let some of the air out of the tires, out of plain desperation. It worked and we got home without any mishaps.

Even the ice helped us to understand how vulnerable we as human beings are and how dependent we were on God for everything.

Blessing Number 33.   The Bank helps

It was ten months since we signed the deal with Billy Gann for the house and all the time I would have preferred it if we were owing the money to a bank rather than to an individual. I decided one day to try my luck and approach the local branch of First Federal Savings and Loan for a mortgage loan, hoping to get something lower than the 9% we were paying Billy Gann. The lady referred me to their main branch in Fort Payne and to a lady by the name of Diane Shanckles.

Diane was as close to an angel, as what we could find on earth. She listened carefully to my story and did everything a person will not normally expect from a bank - she even faxed First National Bank in South Africa to got a credit reference on me and within a month, the bank lend us the money for our house at 8.5%. We were only 16 months in the country and yet they trusted me enough to help us and I knew that God was still taking care of our lives.

Blessing Number 34.   A permanent job offer

One Friday afternoon, the phone rang at about 5 p.m. and a lady asked to speak to me. When I got to the phone, she asked me if I would perhaps be interested in a loan manager's job. No need to say that the idea sounded very enticing and we agreed on a date for an official interview.

I wanted to know from her where she got my name, and she told me that she got my resume from the First Federal bank manager. I substantiated my story and loan application at the bank with account records from South Africa, as well as a copy of my resume. So, when Jimmy Eberhart, the bank manager saw my resume, he remembered that Pioneer Credit, a finance company where his wife owned some shares, was looking for a manager.

I got the job and told Norman: "I would have been satisfied with a clerk's position but the Lord gave me a general manager's job." He replied: "God does not do anything halfway. He always gives more than what we need." I knew Norman was right.

CHAPTER 12.

LOOKING BACK

It was time to reflect on our adventures and experiences. We were now well established with our own house and good jobs and the children were very much "American kids" by now.

Natalie finished high school with a scholarship at North East College in Rainsville, Alabama, Wayne was enjoying his football career and won the academic award for the football players and Melissa started playing basketball and was preparing herself for cheerleading. They were all honor students and no need to say, mom and dad were very proud and happy.

The children made good friends and some of them became like family in this African house. I liked to tease a bit by telling them that we were hoping to be American citizens one day and that we will then be true African Americans - white ones. We were grateful for these kids who helped our children to recover from having to leave their dearest friends in South Africa. We did not really understand the loss that our children suffered and we were told many times by them:" Please don't ever do that again." Hopefully, we will never have to consider such a move again.

We had often wondered, if we knew ahead of time, whether we would have made this drastic move. The answer has always been the same - yes. We have achieved all the goals we set for ourselves and even more. We may never have learned all the lessons if we had made different decisions in our lives and we may never have received the multiple blessings that the good Lord so richly bestowed upon us.

Initially, we may have been looking for greener pastures. What we found and what we experienced was not always what we envisaged in the beginning. We discovered things about ourselves and about our relationships with God and one another that were new to us. We discovered that the greener pastures may not be the material things but rather the spiritual benefits that one may find.

It is absolute true that one will not get anything of value and appreciate it without having to pay for it. We gave the best that we have when we left our loved ones and our country, but we have inherited a life filled with opportunities. It is now up to us to take each day and explore the next blessing that God has already planned for us.

We often had to walk by faith rather than by sight and that within itself, was possibly the greatest blessing of all. It taught us that nobody could ever rely on tomorrow, unless he or she has the Great Master to lead the way. We came to understand and experience so many of the promises Jesus made and were fortunate enough to have the courage to tell others about it.

CHAPTER 13.

LOOKING AHEAD

We are now American citizens. The kids and even Karen have all graduated from college and pursuing their individual careers. We are enjoying our lives in the States but there are days when we all dearly miss South Africa, our family and our friends. Karen and I have had the pleasure of returning for visits to South Africa but the children have not been able to go yet. They have been busy building their careers and have been successful in doing so. Maybe they can get to go to South Africa as soon as our finances permit.

During our visits to South Africa we have been pleasantly surprised by the growth in the country. It is wonderful to see how the country can thrive and every person live in an environment of freedom. We hope and pray that bad elements will be controlled and this progress be expanded to every individual.

Our lives must still go on and we do not know what tomorrow may bring. What we do know however, is that the same God who took care of us and answered our prayers in such great detail, is still in control and we still need Him as much today and tomorrow and the next day as we have ever needed Him before. We cannot and may not set any goal in our lives which we have not discussed with Him in prayer and then wait on Him to open or close the doors as He sees fit.

Yes, God is in control and so He will always be!